NICHOLAS ROYLE is the author of more than 100 short stories, two novellas and seven novels, most recently *First Novel* (Vintage). His short story collection, *Mortality* (Serpent's Tail), was shortlisted for the inaugural Edge Hill Prize. He has edited seventeen anthologies of short stories, including *The Time Out Book of New York Short Stories* (Penguin), *Murmurations: An Anthology of Uncanny Stories About Birds* (Two Ravens Press) and five volumes of *Best British Short Stories* (Salt). A senior lecturer in creative writing at the Manchester Writing School at MMU and head judge of the Manchester Fiction Prize, he also runs Nightjar Press, publishing original short stories as signed, limited-edition chapbooks.

Also by Nicholas Royle:

NOVELS
Counterparts
Saxophone Dreams
The Matter of the Heart
The Director's Cut
Antwerp
Regicide
First Novel

NOVELLAS
The Appetite
The Enigma of Departure

SHORT STORIES
Mortality

ANTHOLOGIES (AS EDITOR)
Darklands
Darklands 2
A Book of Two Halves
The Tiger Garden: A Book of Writers' Dreams
The Time Out Book of New York Short Stories
The Ex Files: New Stories About Old Flames
The Agony & the Ecstasy: New Writing for the World Cup
Neonlit: Time Out Book of New Writing
The Time Out Book of Paris Short Stories
Neonlit: Time Out Book of New Writing Volume 2
The Time Out Book of London Short Stories Volume 2
Dreams Never End
'68: New Stories From Children of the Revolution
The Best British Short Stories 2011
Murmurations: An Anthology of Uncanny Stories About Birds
The Best British Short Stories 2012
The Best British Short Stories 2013
The Best British Short Stories 2014
Best British Short Stories 2015

THE ART OF THE NOVEL

Edited by

Nicholas Royle

CROMER

PUBLISHED BY SALT

12 Norwich Road, Cromer, Norfolk NR27 0AX United Kingdom

Printed in Great Britain by Clays Ltd, Elcograf S.p.A.

Typeset in Sabon 10/13

ISBN 978 1 907773 65 5 paperback

5 7 9 8 6 4

CONTENTS

NICHOLAS ROYLE

INTRODUCTION

F OR A NUMBER of years, teachers of creative writing have
been growing steadily more aware of a baffling contra-
diction at the heart of British culture. We have enjoyed this
privileged view precisely because we are also, by requirement,
practising writers and published authors. As reading – or
reading anything other than sub-*Penthouse* letters page fantasy dressed up as erotica – continues to acquire the cachet of
a marginalised activity, writing, on the other hand, is all the
rage. To put it another way, as print and ebook sales decline
– with the regrettable exception of sub-*Penthouse* letters page
fantasy dressed up as erotica – the numbers of people wanting
to write books continue to rise.

Aspiring writers have been able to apply to study for an
MA in creative writing in the UK since Malcolm Bradbury and
Angus Wilson opened the door at the University of East Anglia
in 1970. Many universities eventually followed suit, setting up
creative writing departments, offering MAs and undergradu-
ate degrees, and now some of the MAs are even turning into
MFAs, not forgetting creative/critical PhDs, while writing
courses are also being offered by publishers, newspapers,

literary agencies and, quite likely by the time this book is printed, breweries, supermarket chains and global internet giants. Predating even UEA, of course, though not offering academic qualifications, were John Fairfax and John Moat, founders of Arvon, who started running residential courses for wannabe writers in 1968, long before the word 'wannabe' was first uttered.

But this book is not just for students of creative writing. It's for readers, for readers of novels, for readers curious about novels and maybe curious about writers, for other writers, maybe short story writers or poets or scriptwriters who want to write novels, for other novelists who might feel a need to hit the refresh button, to pick up some tips, for novelists who are also teachers of creative writing. We never stop learning how to write better or how to improve our teaching.

All the contributors are practising novelists; more than half of them are also, or have been, teachers of creative writing. Each contributor writes about a different aspect of writing novels; some are extremely practical, while others tend more towards the inspirational. Some do both. A typical chapter consists of an original article or essay followed by a favourite creative writing exercise, three top tips and a list of ten novels that may or may not reflect the subject of the essay. I have edited, for the most part, with a light hand, which is not to say I've tolerated missing commas or incorrectly used semi-colons, but within the general structure described above I have allowed a degree of latitude. For instance, the lists of novels look different. Some contributors have taken me at my word and provided a simple list, while others have annotated them, and rather than strip out their annotations or demand commentary from those who didn't add any, I decided to allow variety to prevail, as it does in these writers' novels.

One writer calmly discusses a novel I have implicitly

attacked in this introduction; another contributes an exercise that seems at odds with what I regard as the only way to write fiction, long or short, which is forever to be withholding information. But I have resisted the temptation to interfere in such cases, since it's quite possible they're right and I'm wrong, or that there is no right and wrong. The tone, generally, is informal, even chatty, not that of the academic essay with complicated referencing and endnotes, although there is, as there should always be, one notable exception.

We have not tried to cover everything. We haven't devoted chapters to every genre or every skill, to every technique or element of the novel. There's a chapter that dwells on matters mostly away from the writing desk and there's a chapter that focuses with intense concentration on a single sentence. The fact is it's good to hear a multiplicity of voices, to consider different approaches; that's what this book is all about. Actually, what it's really all about is me getting hold of a bunch of fresh exercises to use next time I'm at tutoring at Arvon's Lumb Bank or Scotland's equally wonderful creative writing centre, Moniack Mhor.

In the spirit of giving something back, here is my favourite creative writing exercise. I have only done it once, with a group of MA students from MMU on a residential week at Moniack Mhor.

Ask your group to come to the workshop with a good pair of shoes and a problem – a problem in their work in progress, rather than in their life more generally. Go around the table and ask everyone to talk a little bit about their problem. Then ask them all to go outside, to split up and to walk for an hour and talk to themselves, out loud, about the problem. By the time they return and sit around the table again, most if not all of them will have resolved their problem.

Out of my group, one stayed behind, possibly unconvinced

by what he might have perceived as my maverick approach. Out of the others, all bar one resolved their problem and the one who didn't came up with a workaround that meant it wasn't a problem any more. Later, the student who hadn't gone said he wished he had. He is now a published novelist and one of the contributors to this book.

Would you like to know my top tips? I'll tell you anyway.

- The hardest thing to get right, assuming you know how to punctuate a sentence, is the balance between saying too much and not saying enough. I would always advise erring on the side of not saying enough.
- Always read your work out loud before you consider it finished.
- Agents and editors are constantly on the lookout for two things – a reason to carry on reading and a reason to stop reading. It's important you give them lots of one and none of the other.

It's also important, though, not to become too anxious around these possible reasons-to-stop-reading, in case this anxiety discourages the taking of risks, and the risks that you do take may very well end up being your reasons-to-carry-on-reading.

You might argue that all novels take risks, and you might be right. But I suppose there are risks and *risks*.

A final self-indulgence, then (it seems only fair on my contributors, of whom I have demanded in each case a list of ten, and I know that some of them, probably all of them, have sweated over these lists): ten novels that I have read more than once (and not for professional reasons). (To spare my contributors' blushes, I am excluding their own work.)

The Blindfold by Siri Hustvedt
Days Between Stations by Steve Erickson
The Glamour by Christopher Priest
Ice by Anna Kavan
Blind Needle by Trevor Hoyle
The Driver's Seat by Muriel Spark
Jealousy by Alain Robbe-Grillet
Fermentation by Angelica Jacob
Nightshade by Derek Marlowe
A Matter of Life and Sex by Oscar Moore

LEONE ROSS

HOW TO WRITE
MAGIC REALISM

Or

HOW TO WRITE WEIRD SHIT

I WILL ALWAYS remember the first time I read Roald Dahl's *James and the Giant Peach*. There was über-orphan James, destined to chop logs for the evil Aunties Sponge and Spiker for all eternity, until one trip and a fall, and hey presto: a gargantuan peach in the back yard. It's the same tension in *Alice's Adventures in Wonderland* – getting on with normal life she was, until a rabbit with a watch came hurrying along and things were never the same again.

When I was a kid, it was that 'trip and fall into weird shit' moment that most delighted me: that gleeful gearshift from everything being pretty darn normal into a world of life-sized insects or chocolate waterfalls. There were other books, but I reserved a very special place in my heart for the *particularity* of the weird invading the normal. Established worlds of fairies and monsters didn't give me the same pleasurable jolt.

Science fiction always seemed a bit cold and organised. It was when the weird got plumped down into the *middle* of everyday life that I was happiest. It seemed the most delicious kind of joke.

As a kid, I didn't know that what I loved was magic realism.

As adolescence beckoned, my relationship with the weird was stalled, in part by a post-colonial, Jamaican education. *Wuthering Heights* and *Great Expectations* offered their own kind of grotesque pleasure, alongside Caribbean masterworks of realism like Naipaul's *A House For Mr Biswas* and Claude McKay's *Banana Bottom*. Outside of school, I dabbled in my mother's well-worn *Dune* series, became a Trekkie, read and re-read *Conan the Barbarian* comics, *The Communist Manifesto* and *Asterix*. None of these provided that fall-down-the-rabbit-hole jolt, but I'd decided that was something you only got from kids' books. I was older now, and Stephen King's gore would have to suffice. Until my first week at the University of the West Indies. Until the moment I picked a random book out of the pile I'd bought for my lit/social science degree and opened it.

'The North Carolina Mutual Life Insurance agent,' I read aloud, 'promised to fly from Mercy to the other side of Lake Superior at three o'clock.' I sat upright. Yes, heart thumping. '". . . I will take off from Mercy and fly away on my own wings,"' I read on. '"Please forgive me. I loved you all."'

It was the first paragraph of *Song of Solomon* by Toni Morrison. I had never heard of her before. A woman? A black woman writing weird shit? And hidden in that same tower of books was another revelation: Gabriel Garcia Marquez's *One Hundred Years of Solitude*. Suddenly I was back in the belly of the odd, but the weird shit I'd almost forgotten was adult-flavoured this time. I was eighteen years old and I didn't know you could *do* that. It would be the twin brilliance and mischief of Morrison and Marquez that would give me permission to begin to write and publish my own weird shit.

So how do you do it, especially if you're not a Nobel prizewinner?

The first thing to remember about 'magic realism' is that it works by mixing the magical or fantastical with reality – *as if it's no biggie*. In these kinds of books, magical bits are included in a straightforward, matter-of-fact manner, often drawing on folk tales and myth. In Erin Morgenstern's 2011 *The Night Circus*, the world seems normal enough until page nine, when a young girl's distress causes a hot cup of tea to break and then re-form. In the novel I'm finishing now, *This One Sky Day,* my protagonist seems to be in a perfectly ordinary world until he wakes up with an erection – and a ghost sitting on his chest, foraging up his left nostril. But neither of these novels is horror, or a ghost story. The skill – and the difference – is not to freak out when the magic comes – or to let your characters freak out either. The father of the kinetic girl in *The Night Circus* doesn't run shrieking to the government. He shrugs and thinks she might be interesting. My character is merely irritated by the ghost; it is the season for them and what he needs is an exterminator.

In magic realism, odd events need not have an explanation, and even if they do, the oddness is fast accepted and adjusted to. There's an important reason for that: in this genre, the extraordinary is tangible and accessible – even marginal. The extraordinary is ordinary. Marquez said he couldn't find his own writing voice until he began to tell strange tales the way his grandmother told them: 'brick-faced', as if they'd really happened. No one thought her mad. Nigerian writer Ben Okri rejects the term magic realism to describe his own work, arguing that the phrase imbues the literature with a kind of 'otherness', a self-consciousness that suggests secularism is the superior 'norm'. I agree. Critic Matthew C Strecher's definition of magic realism as a genre that 'invades' a 'realistic' setting with 'something too strange to believe' is pretty hilarious. Like Okri, I grew up in a country where weird shit isn't so strange at all. The arrival of large black moths *are* messengers from the dead and everybody mutters that truth under the veranda lamp; widows still wear red underwear in some rural areas to prevent horny, dead exes from taking advantage at night. Oh, and if you dream fish, somebody's bound to be pregnant.

Many human communities experience the magical or supernatural as an important part of reality, a way to understand the world. Which is why I tell my students that to write like this, they needn't look further than the myths and legends of their own communities. Thus encouraged, an Irish student immediately recalled his grandfather, an agnostic in every other context, who nevertheless insisted that as a boy, he'd watched a hare get up out of his mother's soup pot, slip back into the bloody pelt discarded on the kitchen table, and jump through the window to freedom.

'We like to think that the world is rational and precise and exactly how we see it,' argues Okri, 'but something erupts in our reality which makes us sense that there's more to the fabric of life . . . Nobody has an absolute reality.'

Given all this, I suggest new writers of magic realism resist the urge to explain everything. Sci-fi and fantasy love to explain, but there is supposed to be an enigmatic element to magic realism, a *something* that cannot be explained by logic. Writer and editor David Young suggests readers treat magic realism as a kind of 'pleasant joke' on realism. I like to think of the genre as a return to child-mind, to mischief, play, awe and wonder.

There are lots of worthy and interesting academic squabbles

about the differences between magic realism and other sub-genres, but frankly, I advise writers to ignore them – for now. The most important thing is to get in the habit of establishing the world of your story as a normal place we all recognise – and then to introduce the strange or fantastical, all casual like. Don't try to explain the weird shit to your readers with science or history or psychology; don't make your characters mad to excuse their 'odd' experiences. This takes a little practice, so you're going to have to read a lot. Start with short stories, even if your ambition is novel writing. Accept it when Italo Calvino describes a boat of men and women attaching a ladder to the moon to gather moon cheese; accept that in Virgilio Piñera's *Meat*, men eat their own mouths, then walk around with the bloody holes gaping. These details are not random or merely amusing: magic is used in this kind of writing to punctuate emotional moments or emphasise an important thematic or plotting point. The work is metaphorical and symbolic.

On the other side of the equation, magic realism harnesses what Russian critic Viktor Shklovsky called 'defamiliarisation'. In his famous essay, 'Art as Technique' Shklovsky urged the artist to find ways to express everyday objects and experiences as new ('estrangement'). We get used to seeing things a certain way: a loaf of bread, a carpet, a dog, a tree. Our perception becomes automatic. Shklovsky said the purpose of art was to remind us to look again. Many works of magic realism specialise in making the everyday even better than the magic. In *One Hundred Years of Solitude*, Macondo villagers are entranced by ice brought by travelling 'gypsies' because they have never seen it before; as readers, we are reminded that frozen water is truly amazing.

There's a final reason why magic realism delights me. Its unique power comes from its hybridity, or fusion. As Okri and Young point out, in *mixing* reality and magic, we insist that both elements are important. This is an unapologetic reclamation, in the best tradition of resistance. The genre is full of stories that include a meeting of two worlds or two power structures – one in touch with magic, the other aligned to the 'real', the provable, the 'norm'. In Katherine Dunn's seminal and astonishing 1989 novel *Geek Love*, a couple breed their own freak show, including the telekinetic Fortunato, who, among many other things, impregnates his sister with their brother's sperm by moving it with his mind. Dunn wanted to explore the idea that a 'symmetrical, common notion of perfection' was ultimately a lie. In this oddball family, strangeness is a good thing and the whole novel presents an inversion of 'traditional' values. If you're just starting out, you may find it helpful to ask yourself what happens when different groups collide, or intersect – and how power dynamics are challenged. I set *This One Sky Day* on a fictional island (probably in the Pacific Ocean) where it's perfectly normal to be born with magical powers, but abnormal to *sell* that magic: where the very earth and sky object when magic dolls are sold to European markets for obscene profit. It is the capitalism that is evidence of a community gone strange; the detachable vaginas, feats of strength and talking goats are ordinary, even boring. Magic realism challenges the reader to ask important questions: what is valuable? Who is right? Who has the power to visit their truth on another? How do we live?

When you finish a good magic realist novel, you shouldn't be able to say what is real and what is 'made up', where fact begins and oddness ends. When you get to the end, you might be tempted to run back to 'logic' once more, but as French critic Tzvetan Todorov says, 'in stories of this kind, the reader must hesitate . . .' Yes, hesitate, as you climb out of the rabbit hole and dust yourself off. Is that a large, magic peach in the sky? Or is it a cloud? And which one is the miracle?

EXERCISE

The Ordinary into the Extraordinary

(a) Write about an actual 'weird' or extraordinary event. This could be a memory, or something you overheard, or read about. Don't explain it, or get logical about it.

Example: when I was 11, I got caught in a burning house. All the doors were locked and the windows were covered with iron 'burglar bars'. I ran through the house, the furthest away I could get from the fire. There was a single opening left, also covered with burglar bars. My mother pushed my father and several firemen out of the way, reached forward and wrenched the bars out of white stone, before dragging me through a space so small I shouldn't have been able to fit. My arms and shoulders were bruised for days and I kept forgetting to breathe properly. My mother shrugs when you remind her: she hardly remembers.

(b) Write about an ordinary person that you know. Establish who they are, what they do, what they like, how they behave. Then give this real person one 'fantastical' or exaggerated trait in order to show us another part of their personality.

Suggestions: your best friend cries blue ink instead of water (writer with creative blocks); your new baby cousin floats if not tied to the bottom of his crib (joy); your grandmother has no shadow (ethereal).

TOP TIPS

- Throw in the 'magic/fantastical' elements to make a point. Kafka used transformation in *The Metamorphosis* to comment on family limits and the nature of humanity.

Okri used a spirit-child protagonist in *The Famished Road* because the concept is perfectly normal within Nigerian traditional religions. My story, *The Woman Who Lived in a Restaurant*, tells the tale of a restaurant that is jealous of its owner's girlfriend, but what it's really about are the sacrifices we are willing to make to be loved, and about love coming in many forms.

- You can use a sprinkling of the fantastic, or go the whole (flying) hog. Don't feel the need to ram some oddness onto every page. The amount of weird can run the scale from pure magic to stories only slightly flavoured with strangeness. You're writing a novel, and a bad story, one-dimensional characters, scrappy structure, the wrong point of view, ineffective dialogue and anything else gone wrong, cannot be disguised by draping it all in weird shit.

- Use all your senses to explore the ordinary around you. Marvel at electricity, planes, butterflies, the whorls on your fingers. Listen to your heartbeat. Give someone you love a massage, and examine their skin, be fascinated by the symmetry of their bones. Be a kid again: pretend you've never seen a banana before. Be an alien, watching human love or rage or digestion – what might shock or amaze you? Go for long walks and look at nature.

TEN BEST MAGIC REALIST NOVELS OF ALL TIME

One Hundred Years of Solitude by Gabriel Garcia Marquez
Song of Solomon by Toni Morrison
The Baron in the Trees by Italo Calvino
Geek Love by Katherine Dunn
The Kingdom of This World by Alejo Carpentier
The Magic Toyshop by Angela Carter
The Night Circus by Erin Morgenstern

Midnight's Children by Salman Rushdie
The Famished Road by Ben Okri
Texaco by Patrick Chamoiseau

TOM BROMLEY

ON COMIC FICTION

THE QUICKEST WAY to kill a joke is to dissect it. The fastest way to suck the joy out of a comic novel, therefore, is probably to analyse what it is that makes it funny. As the late Bob Monkhouse might have put it, when I said I was going to explain what makes comic fiction tick, they all laughed. Well they're not laughing now.

Literary types look down erroneously on all sorts of genre writing, but comic fiction is the one that gets the hardest of Paddington stares. Maybe that's because trying to make the reader laugh is seen as a frivolity compared to the heavy lifting of writing a Proper Book. Maybe it's because in some respects, it isn't even really a proper genre at all: rare is the bookshop indeed where the comic novel gets its own shelf space, like crime or sci-fi. As a genre, the comic novel is either defined so widely as to seemingly include any book with a humorous passage within, or narrowly enough to be seen as a sort of paperback Shakespearean play, the ones where the plots creak with identical twin siblings and hilarious characters called Bottom.

Yet the art of writing a good piece of comic fiction is something that should be celebrated, rather than dismissed. Not only is being able to make the reader laugh a wonderful thing in itself, but from a craft point of view, this is a form of writing that requires much precision and dexterity to pull off. It's a skill, too, that is eminently transferable. Whatever it is you're writing, an understanding of the art of humorous fiction is a great asset to be able to draw on.

Comic fiction is a different kind of comic writing to other forms of humorous material. With a comic novel, there's no studio audience present to ham up to or a canned laughter soundtrack to be added in. Laughter is contagious, but reading is a one-on-one experience. To get someone to guffaw from the printed word alone is a harder task.

On top of which, there's the sheer length of time that a fiction writer has to deal with. How long does it take the average person to read a book? Depends how quick they read or how long the book is, of course. But let's say, for argument's sake, three to five hours. That's probably on the short side, but even so, it's a comparatively long time to consistently make someone laugh. This isn't a ten-minute skit or a stand-up routine. Or a thirty-minute sitcom on the telly. Or even a ninety-minute romcom at the cinema.

To keep someone laughing over such an extended period of time requires comic writing of a different sort of calibre. The clue lies in the name: comic fiction. For a comic novel to work, it has to be both comic *and* succeed as a novel. It can't just be about playing it for laughs. In fact, I'd go further than that: it can't really be about making jokes – not the obvious ones with puns and punchlines and cymbal splashes at the end. That might work over a shorter time frame, but a rat-tat-tat of one-liners over many chapters would fast become tiresome and exhausting to read. Where comic novels often fall down is not that they're not funny, but because they read like a group of sketches and set pieces glued together, rather than a properly rounded work of fiction.

A good comic novelist – and this might sound counter-intuitive – is the one who doesn't try to be funny. Rather, a properly funny author finds their comedy in the fiction itself. It's a subtler blend of humour, more sophisticated (in technique at least) and one that is built to sustain over the course of a narrative. A decent writer derives their comic material from all aspects of the novel, but three in particular stand out: characterisation, dialogue and situation.

HUMOUR FROM CHARACTER

It's striking looking over some of the great comic novels just how many are marked by memorable characters – heck, the likes of Bridget Jones, Jeeves and Lucky Jim reinforce the point by getting their names into the title. Certainly, the seam of humour that can be riven from a memorable protagonist is a rich one to mine.

One of my favourite comic creations is Ignatius J Reilly, the lead character in John Kennedy Toole's wonderful *A Confederacy of Dunces*. It's a book that I've found, from teaching over the years, that splits readers right down the middle: many love it, others can't stand it. That difference of opinion pretty much comes down to the larger-than-life protagonist who dominates proceedings with a 'fleshy balloon' of a head and a dress sense that 'suggested a rich inner life'. Ignatius is the sort to tell a policeman to 'kindly go away', and whips the said officer by a lute string when he doesn't. He's Cartman from *South Park* with a degree in Medieval Studies and every bit as brash, off-the-wall and hilarious as that makes him sound.

But comic characters don't have to be so, well, big-boned.

Nigel Williams is an expert at crafting Ignatius' opposite: the quietly comic individual. Take Henry Farr, the protagonist in *The Wimbledon Poisoner*, a man who decides to kill his wife because 'he could think of no way of prolonging her absence from him indefinitely'. Farr is not a natural killer – he has worries as to whether he can be both a 'red-blooded Englishman' and a 'cold-blooded psychopath' at the same time, and decides that if he is caught, 'being a convicted murderer had the edge on being a solicitor'. You wouldn't be able to miss Ignatius. You probably wouldn't even notice Henry Farr. But both types of character offer an author a world of humour to play with.

HUMOUR FROM DIALOGUE

Dialogue works particularly well for comic fiction, and especially so in romantic comedy: that back-and-forth repartee of (star)crossed purposes offers a quick-fire way of injecting humour and pace into a story at the same time. Helen Fielding is an expert at this: *Bridget Jones' Diary* might be a couple of decades old now, but it is striking how well the writing and dialogue still hold up. The scene near the beginning where Bridget meets Mark Darcy at a family Christmas party is a good example. Everything Mark says, Bridget is wrong-footed by: asked if she is reading anything, Bridget says feminist treatise *Backlash* to end the conversation, only to discover that he has read the book and starts questioning her (who hasn't) about 'special pleading'. When Mark offers her 'my car' to take her back to London, Bridget sarcastically quips 'all on its own?' before finding out Mark has a company car and chauffeur. In an increasingly desperate exchange, Bridget tries to persuade Mark to take a canapé – 'Stuffed olive? . . . Silverskin onion? . . . Beetroot cube?' Throughout, Fielding contrasts Bridget's long, rambling answers with Mark Darcy's short, abrupt responses to capture their characters. It's extremely tight comic writing, with not a word wasted.

Rachel Joyce's *The Unlikely Pilgrimage of Harold Fry* begins with a different sort of conversation between a couple – this time, long-standing husband and wife, Maureen and Harold. It's breakfast time and Harold has just received a letter from an old friend, Queenie. As Harold reads, the couple talk across each other: ('Could you pass the jam?' 'She was in finances.' 'That's the marmalade, Harold. Jam is red.'). Then comes the kicker: Queenie has cancer. It's a darker sort of punchline, but one that employs a comic set-up to deliver it, and also expertly uses the humour in the build up to maximise the scene's impact.

HUMOUR FROM SITUATION

The scenario itself, when set up right, can also really deliver in terms of comedy. Jonathan Coe is an expert at this, particularly in sowing the seeds earlier in a scene and then finishing the moment off in style. In *The Rotters' Club*, Coe deftly describes the horror of a school swimming lesson: any pupil forgetting their trunks, like lead character Benjamin, faces the humiliation of swimming in the nude.

Coe undercuts this seventies sort of school discipline with Chapman, a boy so well-endowed he forgets his trunks on purpose. Having put that in the background, Coe then brings up a second swimming lesson punishment: anybody messing around has to stand on the top diving board for five minutes. Bringing the episode to a close, Coe pulls the two separate punishments together in one memorable scene: a naked Chapman on the diving board, 'clearly visible . . . to anyone travelling on the top deck of a 61, 62 or 63 bus'. Finally comes a wonderful pay-off line: 'During the course of that day the Chief Master had received four complaints, and one request for Chapman's telephone number.'

The whole set-up is just a few paragraphs long: yet the detail, focus and delivery are assiduously done. There's no dialogue here, and no characterisation bar the comparison of Chapman's 'legendary instrument' to 'an airport-sized Toblerone'. The humour here is all in the setting: when done right, as here, it is a winning combination.

These are just three ways that great comic writers ply their trade. Of course, although I've picked out some specific examples, a good writer will draw on a mixture of all these different types of humorous techniques. But whatever your own comic strengths, the more you can embed the humour into the texture of the novel, the more natural it will be.

While all these examples derive their humour in different ways, what they all have in common is the precision of their writing. The comedy comes from the exact placement of the right word, at the right moment, at the right point in the sentence, at the right rhythm, to upset the reader's expectation and make them laugh. That doesn't happen by chance, but because of careful crafting, editing and re-editing until the line is exactly right. The secret of TIMING a good joke is, as they say.

EXERCISE

Write a scene that draws on three elements of comic fiction writing: humour from character, dialogue and situation.

Firstly, create a comic character who is a waiter or waitress at a restaurant. Is he or she larger than life, à la Ignatius J Reilly, or quietly comic like Henry Farr? Secondly, imagine two people coming to the restaurant to have a business lunch. There is some underlying friction between them: show this in the dialogue. Thirdly, when the meal arrives, imagine that there is something surprising or wrong with it. Use this setting as your source of humour to close the piece with.

Aim to write about 500 words. And remember: once you've written your first draft, the hard work of rewriting to wring out the humour really begins.

TOP TIPS

- Rewrite, rewrite, rewrite. This can't be stressed enough in comic fiction. A good comic writer will have worked and reworked the text until every word is in precisely the right place. That involves patience and focus and an appreciation of just how important the editing part of writing can be – as important as the original inspiration.

- Don't tell jokes. Resist the temptation to think that writing comic fiction is about writing jokes. Laughter lines in a novel are more about utilising the characters, the dialogue and the settings: combining the humour with the components of the narrative, rather than just being funny for the sake of it.

- Use light and shade. Humorous writing doesn't have to be light and fluffy. If you add a bit of darkness into the mix, the contrast can actually heighten things. So even if you are writing something overtly funny, don't be afraid to touch on larger subjects; it might just be the making of your piece.

TEN GREAT COMIC NOVELS

John Kennedy Toole, *A Confederacy of Dunces*

Nigel Williams, *A Life Closed Twice*
Helen Fielding, *Bridget Jones' Diary*
Jonathan Coe, *Expo '58*
Kingsley Amis, *Lucky Jim*
Michael Frayn, *Skios*
Evelyn Waugh, *Scoop*
Lucy Ellman, *Man or Mango*
Guy Bellamy, *The Secret Lemonade Drinker*
Rachel Joyce, *The Unlikely Pilgrimage of Harold Fry*

JENN ASHWORTH

LIFE WRITING / WRITING LIFE

1. ON NOT MAKING IT UP

THE POINT OF literature is truth and authenticity. You need to tell it like it is. Rooting your work in personal experience will give you authority: the best stories are true stories, and fiction is fakery. No life, no matter how ordinary and circumscribed, is ever really boring: not if you examine it closely enough. Each of you knows something both unique and significant, even if you don't yet have the confidence to recognise it. They say we've all got a novel in us. Right?

Write what you know.

2. ON MAKING IT UP

Books about domestic suburbia are out. Campus novels are passé. Lightly fictionalised accounts of failing marriages, recoveries from addiction, the finding of lost children and the aftermath of inadequate parenting have all been done before. Research suggests your core market is now resolutely post-realism. They're over it, in other words. Your readers want the improbable and the exotic (perhaps even the far-flung and the far-fetched).

Make it up, for God's sake.

3. ON GOING BEYOND

Forget about what the reader wants, or what people tell you the reader wants, or about what you imagine the reader wants. After the book is published what a reader wants to make of it is none of your business. If she wants to spend time extracting your biography from its pages, that's her look-out. Which shelf a bookseller chooses to display your work on is nothing to do with you right now.

Look at this question – of life writing / writing life – from the writer's side of the desk, which is where we are at the moment. To look at it properly, we might ask another question. Why on earth would anyone want to spend the time it takes to write a novel (years, perhaps?) resting safe in the doldrums of what she knows? When we write about what we know, the writing is dead. It succumbs to second hand language, the cheap laugh, the ease of the familiar stereotype and the counterfeit comfort of a narrative that is hamstrung, limping along a track to confirm as if on autocue what we thought we knew about the world before we started. Writing that begins with a thesis to be shared with the reader is a con-trick – best left to the polemicists and propagandists.

I come across writing like this all the time. Writing that sets out to tell me that losing someone you love hurts, racism is wrong, being a human is confusing sometimes, parenthood can be boring, behind every successful man there is a woman, good people do bad things and other uncomplicated and un-contested truths. I have read dozens of novels that have left me unmoved, my position in the world exactly the same after I finished them as it was when I started them. And I imagine it worked like that for the writers of these novels too, who started with writing what they knew and never allowed the writing process to move them away from it. How might this kind of intellectual and emotional stasis, practised daily, and over time, damage a life?

The word *metaphor* means 'carry beyond' and the language of literary endeavour is one of the ways we can move ourselves (and others, if we're lucky) onwards. We move and are moved by using the work of writing to carry ourselves beyond the limits of certainty and into the unknown. Or to put it another way, writing well about what you know can become a way of uncovering the unknown and the dizzying extent of the unknowable – the mysteries and uncanniness that lurks between the surface of the domestic and the mundane. Especially when we begin with the stories that seem to lie the nearest to us in the murk of our own histories.

Neurologists have demonstrated that when we remember, we don't return to a fixed point in time. We interact with a narrative that displays its colours in a kaleidoscopic image that alters each time we shake it by remembering. Writing from experience, from memory, from the muck and tangle of what lies behind us, is not about retrieving a perfectly formed thing, solid and undisrupted from the sterility of fact as we painstakingly transfer it from life to the page. If that is what it feels like – telling it 'like it was' – you're doing it wrong. Jeanette Winterson has referred to the various fictionalised accounts of her physical, intellectual and imagined experience as dramatised in *Oranges Are Not the Only Fruit* and *Why Be Happy If You Could Be Normal* as remixes and cover versions. David Shields' *Reality Hunger* reminds us that every fact processed by memory is a fiction.

There's a reason why it took ten years of serious writing practice before *The Friday Gospels* – my third novel and the one most obviously rooted in my own experience growing up as a Mormon in a working-class northern market town – was ready to come. I'd tried various Mormon stories before, and they'd fallen flat or crumpled under the weight of their own plots. Hindsight tells me that in my inexperience I thought I already knew the answers to my questions about the restrictive and conservative religious community I'd been born into and since left. I had made up my mind about where I stood on the beauty and danger of faith and family. Writing the novel and allowing the work to move me away from home undid my conclusions and in the end I hope it provides the reader not with an answer to the questions I had, but the apparatus to dismantle their certainties, as it did mine.

Start with what you know if you want to. If there's a story rooted in your own family, your own region, the profession or the faith or the city that you know the best, why not tell it? Find the detail, from memory, research or imagination, and particularise like mad. Tell the story of that day, on that street, in that family. There's no place like home. And there's no place as unhomely as home. Home is like no place. Start with what you know and let the writing carry you beyond it. Writing has a way of keeping you honest about what you don't know – writing well demands precision, the steady hand and the chilly gaze of the surgeon – all the self-serving presumption and emotional short-cutting and cowardly dodging we do when we remember are exposed when we write well about what we remember.

Be prepared.

4. ON THE WRITING LOOP

Even when you write about what you don't know, the writing life has a funny way of becoming circular. The process of research, of interrogating a character's desires, obsessions and fears and making them your own, means that things you invent become things that belong to you. In *Cold Light* I set out to write about a place – Preston – and a situation – the complexity of teenage female friendship – that I thought I knew well. During the process, the 'City' depicted in the novel became a strange, dislocated version of Preston – a version of a city that could be superimposed only imperfectly onto a map. Donald, in *Cold Light*, was a character enchanted by an improbable, ridiculous idea about bioluminescent organisms. I knew nothing about this and, in time, became obsessed by it. Research can become a kind of method-writing, and what starts as a cold-blooded way of collecting factual detail to illuminate a work can become part of the texture of a life. Writing carries you beyond experiences, and constitutes an expansion of experience. Be bold.

5. ON DOUBLES AND THE BALANCING ACT

I've always thought of the best life – which for me is a life that feeds writing, allows it to emerge, and provides the space for it to develop – involves a kind of breathing: reading, conversation, walking, films, music, art and theatre are ways of breathing in – of listening to the conversations the world is having. Writing is one of the ways we have of breathing out, stepping forwards, of joining the debate.

Margaret Atwood, in *Negotiating With the Dead*, describes the doubleness of the writing life. The writer must be at once muse and creator, editor and poet. Must write for the reader, and in complete disregard of the market. Must make it pay, and must avoid selling out. Must cultivate sensitivity and the toughened hide of a rhinoceros. Must practise compassion and ruthlessness. The writing life is one of balance. Remember to breathe in.

It is too easy, especially early in a writing career, to take half-formed works out on the live literature circuit, to hastily publish, to concentrate too hard on the product rather than the process. It takes more patience, more courage, I believe, to construct a writing life that defers the gratification of publication and performance until the work has developed, that devotes as much time to reading and listening as it does to writing. Wait.

6. ON PRACTICALITIES

For most of us, writing is poured into stolen hours between other kinds of work and family responsibilities. Discipline is all. I know a writer who gets up at five in the morning and writes for two hours before her children wake. She goes to bed at the same time as them in order to make that happen. Someone else goes to sleep at eight, sets the alarm for midnight, writes for three hours. I stay up late. Decline invitations. Have never seen *Breaking Bad*.

The writing life is a life of compromise. Writing takes time. More than you think. A thousand words might take thirty hours of work, or more. To write a novel, to have the time in a life to write a novel, other things might have to be sacrificed. It might be the television or social media. It might be the weekend lie in. Make it worth it.

Dorothea Brande in *On Becoming a Writer* recommends a writer schedule writing appointments with herself and keep those appointments with the same diligence and regularity as she turns up at the school gate, or clocks into her paying job each morning. Brande remarks that a writer who finds that her resistance to keep that appointment with the work is overwhelming the desire to write might not be a writer at all. Are the unglamorous hours of a writing life spent at the desk (or for me, in the car during lunch breaks with a biro and a notebook) less appealing to you than the imagined future of having-written?

7. ON BEGINNING

If, when you sit down to begin, you are sweatily convinced that you've bitten off more than you can chew, you will never pull this off, that this project you have in mind is both too exposing, too risky and (somehow) has been done before, to the point of cliché, by too many half-rate keyboard jockeys to mention, but fuck it, you're going to do it anyway, even if it is a waste of time, then you're probably on the way to doing it well. To construct your days around a daily trek into the unknown hinterlands of your life is a privilege, and a choice.

Don't complain. Just begin.

EXERCISE

There's an event that you want to write about. Something that really happened, perhaps to you, or a friend, or a friend of a friend. Find the scene. Isolate the when and where, the detail that will scaffold the story. Why is it important? Did this event constitute an epiphany or a turning point? Was it the moment that everything changed? Write it from the point of view of the main player.

Now turn it around and find another point of view, an alternative perspective. Write it again. What does that event look like now? Do it again. Invent an onlooker or a participant – a character with their own set of imagined motivations and biases. Do it again.

What fresh perspectives and insights, what new ways of looking, has this period of writing opened up to you? Can you write a version of this event that encompasses the possibility of all of them? Could you do this standing outside all of the characters, in the dramatic objective point of view, or by even-handedly breaching the boundary between each of their minds and the reader's? Is there another, better way?

TOP TIPS

- It isn't glamorous to say so, but especially when it comes to writing novels, discipline is as important as talent. Try and work on your draft as often as you can, even if it's just for half an hour a day. It helps to remember that your feelings about the work on any given day are rarely a reliable indicator as to its quality, and it doesn't matter what state your first draft is in; you can always edit it.

- Feedback is important, whether it comes through the rough and tumble of workshop, a creative writing course or a trusted friend. But choose carefully when you'll show your work to others: too early, and you won't have had time to develop your own ideas and intentions. Too late and it won't matter what anyone else says; you won't want to unpick seams and start to rewrite if you consider the project finished.

- Research is an enjoyable part of the process, and sometimes turning up an unexpected fact or detail can alter the course of an entire novel in surprising and interesting ways. But sometimes hours browsing Wikipedia can start to look suspiciously like procrastination. You won't ever know everything, but you're still allowed to write. Find your place of unknowing, begin, and let your first draft teach you what it needs.

TEN NOVELS THAT BREAK THE RULES

William Faulkner, *As I Lay Dying*
Gustave Flaubert, *Madame Bovary*
Kazuo Ishiguro, *The Unconsoled*
Jon McGregor, *Even the Dogs*
Flannery O'Connor, *The Violent Bear It Away*
Keith Ridgway, *Hawthorn and Child*
Muriel Spark, *The Driver's Seat*
David Vann, *Legend of a Suicide*
Kate Walbert, *Our Kind*
David Foster Wallace, *Infinite Jest*

AJ DALTON

NARRATIVE PERSPECTIVE

CONSIDER THE SENTENCE below and decide whether (taken in isolation) it represents 'good' or 'bad' writing:

He spoke to the rebarbative guy.

Answer: it's awful. Our question of course has to be what makes it so bad. Well, it's bad in a whole variety of ways, ways which it is important for any developing writer to appreciate and understand, ways which I shall attempt to describe below.

First of all, *rebarbative* is a word derived from Latin (evident from the length of word, the Latinate prefix *re-* and the Latinate suffix *-ive*), while *guy* is a word derived from Anglo-Saxon (evident from how short it is). Latin-based terms, as used in English, tend to be formal in tone. By contrast, Anglo-Saxon-based terms tend to be informal in tone. Therefore, the two words do not really collocate ('go together'), creating something of a mixed or paradoxical tone (and the Anglo-Saxon-based *spoke* similarly 'jars' with *rebarbative*).

Why has the writer of the sentence in question chosen to drop a big Latin word in the middle of a short Anglo-Saxon sentence then? In order to sound 'literary' probably. Attempting to use long words in writing is something that we are often encouraged to do when we are young (by parents and pedagogues alike) – it is therefore a difficult habit to 'unlearn'. Using long words for the sake of it is self-indulgent, unnecessarily challenging for readers, and a disaster in terms of tone (as previously described). To give you another example, you might ask a friend in Anglo-Saxon 'Can you give me some help?', while you should make a request of someone more official with the Latinate 'Could you provide me with some assistance?'

Next, we have to realise that the adjective *rebarbative* is someone's opinion of the *guy*. Yet whose opinion is it? The subjective opinion does not really belong to the character who is objectively being described as *He*. Instead, then, the opinion appears to belong to some narrator who is objectively watching (and then reporting) events. Yet if there is no consistent sense of the narrator's 'voice' throughout the writing (if the narrator has not been given a name and characterised), the voice can only belong to the author. In this respect, the term *rebarbative* is an example of 'intrusive author voice'. The author is telling us what to think of the guy, rather than showing us the guy's behaviour and allowing us to judge for ourselves. The author is 'getting in the way' of the story and the action. Of course, this style of writing is often known as 'expository'. In terms of modern prose, too much exposition is considered a hallmark of poor-quality writing. 'Show, don't tell!' is the rule of thumb here.

You might be wondering how big a problem 'intrusive author voice' really is in writing. Doesn't every author have their own 'style'? Don't we want to appreciate something of that style? When an author chooses to use a literary device (a metaphor, bathos, litotes, oxymoron, paradox etc), aren't they intruding somehow? Do we really mind the intrusion? Especially when true craft is on display? Actually, it depends on just how intrusive an author is being. An author's voice can be a tantalising ghost that adds mystery and atmosphere to a piece (eg Edgar Allan Poe) or it can be a wailing banshee that dominates and drowns out everything else. It is only with a good degree of self-awareness and practice that a writer learns to moderate/modulate their voice. Just as a singer, no matter their potential and raw talent, needs to learn to breathe and control their notes.

At best then, the sentence in consideration represents technically bad writing ('It doesn't sound natural'). At worst, it alienates a reader to the point that they don't want to read a single sentence more. The reader feels bullied or manipulated by the author. They 'dislike' and 'distrust' the author. It is precisely for this sort of reason that product advertisements using too many adjectives are perceived as 'over-selling' their products.

To test the outlined contentions concerning just how bad the sentence really is, we might try to rewrite the sentence. First we might seek to use an Anglo-Saxon synonym in place of the offending Latinate adjective. That would give us something like *He spoke to the snarling guy* or *He spoke to the stubborn guy*. It 'feels' better, and it sounds more 'natural', but it still leaves us with the potential problem of exposition and intrusive author voice. We need another trick perhaps.

The trick that is often used is to write the sentence in first person: *I spoke to the rebarbative guy*. Now the word rebarbative represents the opinion of the narrator (rather than the author). The selection of this Latinate word helps build the character of the narrator (it suggests the narrator is pompous, condescending or overly privileged). The word is revealing and adds to the drama. The narrator must have a reason for the opinion, be it an earlier moment of drama or something about the guy that creates animosity in the narrator.

Even when first person narration is clumsy and inconsistent in its use of Latin and Anglo-Saxon, still we see it as descriptive of the narrator's level of education or attitude, rather than seeing it as an example of 'bad writing'. First person narration, then, can allow a reader to excuse a multitude of technical sins. A debatable example is *Fifty Shades of Grey*. It is written in first person – opening with a harassed Anastasia struggling to find time for her university assignments while standing in for a friend at short notice who is due to interview the mysterious millionaire Christian Grey. The opening contains examples of poor collocation, mixed syntax, split infinitives and dangling prepositions – but it is extremely successful in showing Anastasia's state of mind. It almost reads as 'stream of consciousness' (a high/macro/extended literary device). We are even able to sympathise with Anastasia, for she is suffering from that most modern of problems: being time-poor. It certainly is an effective writing style.

Is the solution then always to write in first person? Sadly, there are also significant disadvantages when it comes to using first person narration. First of all, the first-person narrator needs to be present at the moment of most important plot points, which can cause some real contortions in a plot or make the plot feel forced. An example of this can be found in Bram Stoker's *Dracula*. The tale is told in great part through the first-person journal entries of Mina. Mina typically spends her time confined to drawing rooms or going on short walks – the scope of her day-to-day life is far too limited to describe the wider doings of the character Dracula, so the novel then has to leap to the journals of other characters, long newspaper articles, and letters written between characters. There is no doubt that the pacing of the story-telling suffers, and there is a loss of dramatic tension because the reader knows the character responsible for each journal entry must always survive any horrific encounter described. As Stephen King puts it in his preface to the 1978 New American Library edition of *Dracula*: '*Dracula* is frankly a palpitating melodrama couched in the badly creaking frame of the epistolary novel.'

So where does that leave us if we wish to avoid the intrusive author voice of *He spoke to the rebarbative guy*, while also wishing to avoid the problems inherent in first-person narration? Should we remove the adjective altogether, so that we are just left with *He spoke to the guy* or even *He spoke to the man*? Well, if every sentence were to start becoming so stative/transactional, our writing would be dry (or very spare) indeed.

The approach that is used in much modern prose is to use third-person narration while making sure that each scene is clearly written from the narrative perspective of that scene's main character. Narrative perspective never shifts from one character to another within the same scene. A very good example is George RR Martin's *A Game of Thrones*. Each chapter is named after a character. Each chapter is told from the third-person narrative perspective of the character after which it is named. It is an approach that allows the reader to follow the main narrative thread by jumping from character to character between chapters. Large plot events can be told from one perspective, and then retold from another. It creates an epic and 360-degree view of events. It allows for a plurality of viewpoint, rather than imposing a single-world view (in the way that old-fashioned 'omniscient narrator' descriptions often do). It is a far more democratic approach to story-telling, one that resonates with modern readers.

Is that the perfect solution then? Not quite. If we think further about *A Game of Thrones*, we might wonder by what strange mechanism it is that the reader is permitted to go from one character's head to another's. It's not like each character has been submitting their journal entries for someone to edit together, after all. Of course, the reader knows it is the author ferrying them from one perspective to another – and in this manner the author is effectively manipulating and interfering. When the author does so clumsily, they risk alienating the reader. Therefore, it is the author's job to be as subtle and discreet as possible when moving the story along.

At the end of the day, there is no perfect formula when it comes to creative writing. It is still as much an art as it is a science. The 'scientific' 'rules' need to be learned and applied, but that isn't enough on its own to create something unique. When we consider the art of it, our art can be good or bad. When it is bad, we can try again. When it is bad, we can try to develop ourselves into better artists. We can try to be better through practice and an awareness of what didn't work last time. The majority only 'master' their art after great practice. Even then, the art still challenges them. Despite all their success, as previously mentioned, EL James and George RR Martin still have to wrestle with narrative perspective, but they have prevailed, because they have practised and discovered what works for them and their readers.

EXERCISE

In the following examples, identify where we have an unfortunate shift in narrative perspective or we have intrusive author voice.

- The sailor wove his way along the quay – in part because the crowds were thick, in part because that was the way his sea-legs moved, and in part because of his recent visit to the inn. A filthy, suspicious-looking, old crone called out to him and – being a helpful and trusting sort – he made his way over to her.

- Given these new complications and the issue of costs increasing in an uncontrolled manner, we would recommend that the management just stop everything.
- Jack's stomach turned over. *Hate this. Not even sure I want the damn job. Look at these people.* The kindly woman leading the interview panel smiled and wondered at Jack's angry frown.

TOP TIPS

- Make sure each scene in your writing is told from a single narrative perspective. Do not shift between perspectives in the same scene. Make the perspective being used to describe each scene clear from the start. Perhaps name the character. Perhaps immediately tell us something they see and something they think.
- When using an adjective in your writing, check that it represents the 'opinion' of the character whose perspective is being used to describe the scene.
- Be consistent in your use of Latin-based language and Anglo-Saxon-based language. Be particularly wary when combining them. Perhaps associate Anglo-Saxon with certain characters (eg common workaday types) and Latin with others (eg official or upper class types).

BOOKS YOU MIGHT WISH TO CONSIDER IN TERMS OF NARRATIVE PERSPECTIVE APPROACH

For Whom the Bell Tolls, Ernest Hemingway – the master of stative, journalistic prose.

Moby-Dick, Henry Melville – with the famous opening line 'Call me Ishmael.'

The Curious Incident of the Dog in the Night-time, Mark Haddon – excellent example of first person narrative.

The Collected Tales and Poems, Edgar Allan Poe – haunted and haunting prose.

The Lord of the Rings, JRR Tolkien – with an omniscient narrator that indulges in extended description based on a single-world view.

Animal Farm, George Orwell – with an omniscient narrator who uses spare, stative prose.

Wolf Hall, Hilary Mantel – told in third person, but also present tense!

A Game of Thrones, George RR Martin – to see how a plurality of viewpoint might be used.

Dracula, Bram Stoker – to see how even this classic struggles with a framework for its various narrative perspectives.

Fifty Shades of Grey, EL James – to see how a first-person narrative perspective can excuse a multitude of 'sins'.

NIKESH SHUKLA

GO DO IT

WHEN YOU'VE GOT a job, kids, degree or Netflix, writing a novel feels like the impossible dream. When you've got a smartphone, you've got no time or space for imagination to creep in; you've got Twitter.

With a world filled with distractions how are you going to get those 1,000 words done? I hear you. I've written six novels on a full-time job. I've had a baby. I've diversified into TV and theatre. I also have Netflix. I love arsing about on Twitter. So how have I written six novels? Well, through motivation. We'll get to that. Firstly, a disclaimer: out of the six novels I've written, only two of them were publishable. One other is currently being made good. Builders have this euphemism for fixing stuff or mending things or decorating over issues. They 'make good' a problem. That's what's happening with my third official not-stuck-in-the-metaphorical-drawer-of-my-hard-drive novel.

Malcolm Gladwell has this rule about it taking roughly 10,000 hours to be good at something. If you practised one hour a day for 10,000 days, it'd take you well over 13 years to do it. Which doesn't help when you've got that novel burning

a hole in your brain's pocket. It takes time, sure. And a lot
of writing tips give you the whole 'write 1,000 words a day'
spiel, which is totally attainable. I believe in that. And that's
fine. But the reality is, 1,000 words a day sometimes feels piss
easy. Other days, it feels like a struggle. Most days, it feels
like a chore. Some days you may even forget. Other days you
could find yourself in the pub. Yesterday, you slept through
your alarm. Tomorrow Paul's coming round to watch *Better
Call Saul*. So, how you're going to keep those writing muscles
excited and working for 13 years is questionable. Thirteen
years of learning guitar seems feasible, because much as your
tastes in music may change or stray, you're still learning by
playing other people's things. You don't learn to write by rewriting *The Great Gatsby* or *Pride and Prejudice*. Your 10,000
hours are spent, from the get-go, creating brand new things,
rather than practising other people's work till your fingers
bleed.

And that can really mess with your motivation. Right?

I wrote *Meatspace* on the bus, which was quite a feat. I'd
moved to Bristol. I commuted to London on the 5.45am bus
and back on the 6pm bus two days later. I remember once
reading Lee Rourke and Jon McGregor talking about note-
books on Twitter. They were both discussing, along with
Niven Govinden, the need to write each word down. The
penstroke and the analogue feel of the word breathing,
birthing, living, was important to their process. I thought
. . . who has the fucking time? By hand, I write so fucking
slowly.

Meanwhile, I spend a lot of time at my computer, typing. I
spend a lot of time on my phone, typing. I'm good at typing,
and I don't have a lot of time. Also, typing means you can
switch between the Word-document-of-work-you're-meant-
to-be-doing and your novel without arising much suspicion.

So fuck all that romanticising of the written word – just write. It's never been easier to do so.

It's easy. Find the time to write. If you want to write, you'll find the time to do it. If you're motivated to TCB (take care of business – I used the acronym to save time (I realise this is ridiculous, seeing as I'm over-explaining this to you (imagine how many words you could have written instead of reading this bit))), you'll not be distracted by the internet and you'll use your time. Know how I do it? I get up early every day.

It's perfectly reasonable to get up at 6am, write for 90 minutes and then go to my job, write in my lunch break using Google Drive to ensure I have access to the latest draft at all times, then work, then write for an hour in the evening. My friend Josie Long has a system called The Golden Game. She says being busy and being creative are two mutually exclusive things, so the best way to be creative amongst the busyness is to dedicate 90 minutes a day to writing. You have to go out and be creative for 90 minutes. Imagine it's the sports game of your life. For the league or the cup or something. And if you give it your all for 90 minutes you'll achieve as much as you would in a whole day. And you have time to go to your job. There's a little tip.

Also, the fact that I have a job means that my entire life isn't chatting to other writers and people in publishing. It isn't insular. It means I meet different people every day, I observe normal levels of human behaviour and what they really mean. Working with young people means I am always current in my slang. Yagetme? Working in an environment where there are people around means I live in the world I write about.

Imagine me, on my iPad (yes, I wrote *Meatspace*, a book about the ills of social media, on an iPad, in transit on the M4) in transit on the M4, awake only through the power of a Thermos of coffee, and the coughing guy next to me – the one who arrived for the 5.45am bus every day at 5.47am, and was still let on, and always sat next to me – the iPad balanced delicately on my knees. The thing that kept me going was writing in chunks on an iPad makes it hard to go back. You feel the urge to keep moving forward because it's hard to revel in what you've already done.

I wrote the first draft of *Meatspace* in 63 days. And a half. I was so near the end on day 63, I did an extra 45 minutes later that day just to have the pleasure of writing 'FIN' at the end.

Sixty-three days, cramped on a coach on the M4. Sounds easy, right? It wasn't. It was really hard. Because, at 5.45am, it's hard to stay motivated. So, below is my writing plan for writing the first draft. Because the first draft is the scariest draft – it's the draft before anything has been committed to the page. It's the blinking cursor of an empty Word document. The first draft is the hardest draft because there's nothing to make better, nothing to improve, and nothing to hone. Get your first draft done. Waging a war of attrition on your first draft till it's perfect is easier than having an empty document. Because when you have a job or a degree or Netflix, an empty document is much easier to ignore than a completed draft that needs you to edit it into something publishable.

HOW TO WRITE THE FIRST DRAFT OF A NOVEL IN 2.5 MONTHS USING THE SHUKLA METHOD AND THE JOSIE LONG GOLDEN GAME

Rule 1: Move forward. Never revisit. Revisiting is for draft 2.

Rule 2: Draft 1 is the scariest draft because it's an empty page.

Rule 3: Initial rush is followed by malaise is followed by stress is followed by a flurry is followed by doubt about the end.

Rule 4: When you get to a block, write [insert scene where A, B, and C happen. Resolution = ?].

Rule 5: Write at the same time every day. The time when you know you're free. I write 6am-7.30am five days a week. Writing at the same time ensures a routine. According to Oprah, it takes seven days to establish a routine, 30 days to break an addiction.

Rule 6: Play The Golden Game [see above].

So . . .

2.5 months = 25 working days + 25 working days + 13.5 working days = 63.5 days.

In 90 minutes, you can write 1,500 words. If you're playing the best game of football of your life, you're producing 5 x 1,500 words a week.

Let's assume that your minimum is 1,000 words and your maximum is 1,500 words, so on average you are producing 1,250 words a day for 63.5 days.

63.5 days x 1,250 words = 79,375 words. Let's round that up to 80K words in 2.5 months.

Now, that gives you a leeway of 10,000 words because you only really need 70K words for your first draft.

Your first draft is a skeleton. You get those 70K words done, stick it in a drawer for two weeks, then you edit, ten pages a day. And you add and you add. And take away. And rewrite as necessary. You never have an empty page.

2.5 months – 70,000 words. Go do it.

Okay?

EXERCISE

Here's a little palette cleanser I like to do when I'm stuck. It's called Bad Words. Set a clock for one minute. Open up a Word document. Write all the bad words and phrases, all the words you do not want in your book. Just get them out of your system. Treat this separate Word document as the bin. As a show of faith, here are all the bad words I don't want in my next novel, written in one minute. It's 9.04pm right now. I'll see you in one . . .

Very, also, really, amazeballs, iconographer, succulent, moist, poetry-in-motion, jellz, awesome, -gate, -pocalypse, holi-bobs, granular, blue-sky, but, for me, in my opinion . . .

Pretty rank, right? Now . . . do your list of bad words – it'll make it easier to choose the good ones.

TOP TIPS

- Your first draft will never be perfect. That's OK. It's not the draft that'll be published.
- Write at the same time every day. Consciously make time for it. Commit to it like you do meals.
- The abundance of writing tips proves no one knows anything. You know yourself. You'll know when it's good.

BOOKS BY AUTHORS OF COLOUR YOU MAY HAVE NOT SEEN BECAUSE AUTHORS OF COLOUR AREN'T AS VISIBLE AS WHITE ONES

The Intuitionist by Colson Whitehead
Moth Smoke by Mohsin Hamid
Black Bread White Beer by Niven Govinden
The Death of Vishnu by Manil Suri
Saraswati Park by Anjali Joseph
An Untamed State by Roxane Gay
Quicksand and Passing by Nella Larsen
The Lonely Londoners by Sam Selvon
Family Life by Akhil Sharma
We Need New Names by NoViolet Bulawayo
The Village by Nikita Lalwani

STELLA DUFFY

WHAT SORT OF A
BOOK IS IT?

A H, THE PERENNIAL question, and always the chance of
genre snobbery rearing its ugly head. Oh, it's just a crime
novel, just a romance, just chick-lit, lad-lit, mum-lit, misery-
lit, horror, sci-fi, magical realism, women's fiction, commercial
fiction . . .

I am a novelist and short story writer. I've written thirteen
novels and over fifty short stories, along with half a dozen
plays and several solo shows, a few film and television projects. Some of my novels have been sold as crime fiction. Some
of them, not the crime ones, have magical elements, some were
sold as literary fiction, others as commercial fiction. There's
the 'London novel' (several are set in London, but only one
was called a 'London novel'), and the historical novels that
are, depending on the reviewer, termed literary-historical or
categorised by their time period (late Roman, early Byzantine).
There's the fact that the crime novels are often put on the gay
shelf, what with having a lesbian protagonist and booksellers liking to categorise by hero, readers liking to categorise by

type, publishers liking to know the market, and the market loving us all divided up into neat little shelves where we never cross into another's domain.

Except it doesn't actually work like that when I write. What happens is I have an idea. And that idea slowly forms, slowly finds itself, I begin to recognise this half-formed possibility as a book, story, play. Sometimes I realise it isn't actually an idea, it is just a whim, and just because it is a pretty whim doesn't mean I should spend the next two years working on it. Basically, by letting it form before I start work, I begin to understand what it might be. Because what I am is a writer. I have ideas and they become stories and the story dictates the form, the style, the genre.

The question 'what sort of a book is it?' has no place in a book called *The Art of the Novel*. It is welcome in one titled *How to Sell Your Novel* or *What To Say to People at Parties*. But if what you're trying to do, if what we're trying to do, is write the next story that moves us to spend six months, two years, four years writing it, then what kind of a book it is should come far below how it is written, why it is written, with what passion it is written and – for me the most important reason – the story that is calling to be written.

But that's not how publishing works. Publishing is a business. Publishing wants to know what kind of a book we have written (given lead times it actually wants us to know what kind of a book we will write), so it knows what kind of audience to market it to, what type of cover to give it, what form of publicity it needs, what style of author to sell us as. We make the work, publishing assigns it a genre, and then the readers let us both know if we've got it right.

In the mere twenty years that I've been published, the business has changed beyond recognition. I wrote my first novel on an old Amstrad computer and the dot-matrix printer took seven hours to print up a book that was less than three hundred pages long. We have gone from hand-written copy notes to track changes, from bookshop tours to blog tours, and from books to e-books. All of this has driven the speed of creation and manufacture, encouraged us to consider the market before and during as well as after writing, to plan what will happen in six months when we finish writing, when we would ideally be thinking about what is happening now, as we write. And not because the work is so special and glorious, or because the writer is such a profound artist, but out of respect for the reader – without whom we are only one half of the transaction of the novel.

None of this is to say that I believe paying attention to the market is a bad thing. Unless we are writing to put our work away in a drawer or file and never share it, of course we should consider the market. Unless we are writing to disseminate it ourselves and don't care about publishing, traditional or otherwise, of course we should consider the manner of our book sales. But not primarily, and not as a starting point.

I don't teach regularly, the occasional workshop or lecture, an Arvon course most years, but I find it profoundly depressing that at every course there is more than a smattering of people who are there because they truly believe that publishing (publishing!) is a way to make money, that the aim of writing is to make money, and if they can only crack a 'formula' – more often than not involving genre, seeing as they often perceive genre writing to be easier – then all will be well.

This is wrong on so many levels, but let's take them one by one:

Writing fiction is a way to make money. No, it's really not. Writing is a way to do writing. Anything else is about marketing, sales, spin, about the business of publishing. If you want to write in order to sell, then I suggest a fiction writing course is the wrong place for you. Find out about business and write about that. Better sales there too.

The aim of writing is to make money. No. The aim of writing is to tell a story. If you are telling a story with no aim other than to make money, the reader will smell it a mile off, and they will let you know very quickly. Think of yourself as a reader, you can tell when a piece has been written with passion or with cynicism, with drive or with deadline, we all can. Many writers make some money, some writers make great money, but the writers I know who sell hugely well are writing work they enjoy writing, they love what they do, and it shows.

That there is a formula that can be cracked.

(a) if there is, do you think anyone is going to sell that to you for a price we normal people can afford?

(b) if there is, then why hasn't whoever is teaching the 'formula' given up teaching and gone on to make their millions? (Unless, of course, they're making millions from selling you a formula? Always a possibility. They used to call that snake oil.)

(c) there is no formula.

Writing genre is easier. Any writing has its hard and its easy parts, all writing can be easy on a good day and horrendous on a bad one. If you don't deeply understand the genre you're writing in, if you don't love it, if you don't value it, then writing in genre is likely to be one of the hardest things you'll ever do.

I'm not saying that writers shouldn't make money – all artists should be able to make a living, ideally a good one. The idea that artists should create just for the hell of it (and still we so often do) is fine in a society where the only people we want as our artists are the already-wealthy who can afford to create. I want to hear from all people, and all sections of society as writers, as artists, as makers, so yes, artists need to be paid. Ideally well.

I am saying that putting the question of money before the question of what you want to write is dangerous. Not least because none of us can second-guess the market, so even if it was good for your writing (which I think is questionable) to consider 'how much?' before 'what story?', there is no guarantee that the market will not have changed utterly in the weeks, months or years it takes you to create your piece of work. Markets do that, it's how capitalism thrives.

And so to the question genre, of shelves in bookshops, landing pages on websites, and book covers that appeal to one demographic only, a market driven by publishers and readers and booksellers and writers that encourages us to care more about the genre than the story, more about how the product will sell, than how well we can write it.

My books have been on the Crime, Historical, Literary, Women's Fiction (no, I don't know either), and LGBT shelves. I am happy for them to be on all of those shelves, what I'm not keen on is when they are only on one of the shelves at a time. I'm not keen on that because it's bad for sales (see? I do care about sales), I'm not keen on it because it's bad for readers (the wider we read, the wider our world), I'm not keen on it because it's bad for writers.

When I wrote my first novel, *Calendar Girl*, I thought I was writing a novel about a relationship breakup. I thought it was a relationship novel. Because it had a detective in it, it was sold as a crime novel. And because that detective was a young gay woman, it was often put on LGBT shelves. We were all right, but had I set out to write a crime novel or an LGBT novel, I would have written a very different book. I believe *Calendar Girl* was better for the fact that it was written considering story first. I wrote without trying to conform to any genre strictures, which are arbitrary anyway (and often wrong, the same crime genre strictures cannot be applied to Agatha Christie as to Raymond Chandler), I wrote giving primacy to the story, the characters, the plot. The novel was reviewed as new/different/fresh. I didn't set out to conform to a genre and therefore the book, which was sold in two genre 'slots', stood out.

I have many good friends who write genre fiction, most of them hugely successful. I probably know a dozen people who write bestsellers year in, year out. Most of those bestsellers are genre fiction. Most of these people are writing a book a year. Usually that means the whole book, start to finish, including the edit, in nine months or less, to allow three months to do the publicity that sells the book they finished last year. None of them started by looking around for the genre that would get them published or make them the most money, they started writing what they enjoyed reading, what they were moved to write, the stories they wanted to tell. Then they told the story they wanted to tell and found it was also the story the readers wanted to buy. But I don't know a single successful writer – by which I mean a writer who makes their living by selling their work, whether they are bestselling authors or not – who did so by writing material they didn't care about, or by writing books they didn't themselves already read, already find engaging.

Write the best you can for you. Do it with an eye to the reader, thanks for the editors, with hope of the agent and publicists and marketing people and bookshops who will sell you. But for your own sake – write for you.

As writers we only have ourselves to write from, our lives,

our feelings, our dreaming. Writing is a physical activity, we write with our bodies, from our bodies. Even if you're speaking into voice-recognition software, you're still using your body. We have no choice but to write from ourselves, and we do so – with more passion, more guts, more truth, more engagement – when we write for and from the story we are driven to tell. Everything else is secondary. Write for you.

EXERCISE

Sleeping, running, singing, chanting, swimming – anything that lets the conscious mind float free.

TOP TIPS

- Finish the first draft, then make it better.
- Plot is what happens, story is what it means. A good piece of work needs both.
- If you think you can only write in silence/the city/the country/at midnight/at dawn you will stop yourself writing an awful lot of the time. We all have preferred spaces and times to write – make them a preference, not a necessity.

TEN NOVELS THAT MATTER TO ME

JD Salinger, *Raise High the Roofbeam, Carpenters* & *Seymour, An Introduction* (best short story, best writing about writing – and probably both are either novellas or short stories, but they belong in every list, regardless)
Janet Frame, *Owls Do Cry* (lyricism in narrative)
Russell Hoban, *Riddley Walker* ('write what you know' is highly over-rated)
Margaret Atwood, *The Edible Woman*

Barbara Trapido, *Brother of the More Famous Jack*
Mary McCarthy, *The Group*
(All three of the above – women writing about relationships
and friendship – are just as universal as any book by a man
about life and love, but are less likely to be included in a list of
books about the universal – could it possibly be because they
are about women's life and loves . . .?!)
John Irving, *A Prayer for Owen Meany* (it's not about finding
your voice, it's about finding the *story's* voice)
Ali Smith, *Girl Meets Boy* (I love all of Ali's work, this is especially pure and daring)
Hilary Mantel, *Wolf Hall* (I'm happy to admit I find long
books daunting – but every word here was needed, a rare and
precious thing in a novel of many pages)
Patricia Grace, *Tu* (fantastic New Zealand/Aotearoa author,
not nearly well enough known elsewhere)

MARK MORRIS

HOW IMPORTANT IS CHARACTERISATION IN HORROR FICTION?

MANY YEARS AGO I wrote a novel called *The Immaculate*. It was a ghost story about a successful writer who returns to his childhood home after his abusive father's death, and is subsequently forced to deal with the repercussions of his troubled and turbulent past. In contrast to my previous two books, it was a slow-building novel, which relied for much of its impact on how readers would relate to my protagonist, Jack Stone. If they didn't care about Jack and his plight, if they weren't swept along with him on his often frightening emotional journey, then the novel would be dead in the water.

I remember that although my editor at the time enjoyed the book, she was concerned about the lack of 'horror incident'. I remember her using the phrase 'the average horror reader' on several occasions. Her argument was that 'the average horror reader' might not be very interested in all the 'character stuff' in the novel, and might require more shocks, more blood and gore, to keep them reading.

To give her her due, she was a perfectly good editor. The problem was simply that she hadn't read very much horror fiction. Like many non-horror readers, she laboured under the misconception that horror fiction was all about incident, about plot, about ladling on the fluids. But horror fiction is no different to any other type of fiction. The most important aim for any fiction writer is to engage the reader, to make them interested in the story you're telling them. And the only way you can do that is by making them care, or at least interested, in the characters that populate your story.

The reason Stephen King is so successful is because he's a master at this. He takes time to build character, to create back-story. He constantly, though not exhaustively, drops in character notes throughout his narratives – quirks of speech or behaviour, carefully selected background details – that add flesh to his characters' bones, that bring them alive on the page. He often adds touchpoints – character thoughts, opinions, observations – that we, as readers, can at least understand, if not identify with. He gives his characters flaws and foibles; he makes them *human*.

But *how* does he do this? Or to make the question more general, how can we, as writers, do this?

It's very important, when setting out to write a novel, that you plan it properly. Novel preparation can come in the form of copious notes, or it can simply be a case of thinking in depth about the book you're aiming to write before launching in to it. Whatever your method, one aspect – in my opinion, the most important aspect – you must be clear about before you set pen to paper (or fingers to keyboard) are the characters in your story. Too many writers are so enamoured of their *ideas* that they rush ahead without thinking about the characters that are going to carry the story along, as a result of which they end up spoiling the book by populating it with sketchy, unconvincing characters that no one cares about. A potentially dull scene – someone brushing their teeth, for example – can be made interesting if the reader likes and/or relates to whoever is doing the brushing (or at least finds them intriguing). On the other hand, a potentially thrilling scene – a space battle, say – can lie flat and dead on the page if the reader has no emotional investment in the people piloting the space ships, no interest in whether they live or die.

Let's take it as read, therefore, that fiction is at its most engaging, its most compelling, when it is character led. Let's also take it as read that in order to create compelling, interesting characters you have to first put some thought into them.

Here again we come back to the question of *how* writers do this. One thing to bear in mind is that there are no hard and fast rules. All writers are different, and as such have their own methods and approaches that work for them. My own rule of thumb for a successful and convincing character is when they exist *outside* the story, by which I mean, when I, as the writer, know far more about the character than I'll possibly need for the story I'm writing.

It might seem an obvious thing to say, but the way to achieve this is to think about your characters as if they were real people. Don't regard them as plot vehicles, whose existence is bound by the confines of your story. Think about where they were born, who their parents are or were, whether they have brothers or sisters, what kind of childhood they had. Think about who their friends are and where they met them, who they've had relationships with. Think about what they're interested in (books? Music? If so, which writers? Which bands? Movies? What's their favourite film/genre/director?). Think about what they believe in, their philosophy on life, their outlook, their general demeanour.

Once this process starts to work you shouldn't have to

force it. It should flow naturally, and as a result the reactions and responses of your characters, their opinions and emotions, should feel instinctively *right* on the page.

This approach, of course, works for all aspects of fiction, but let's steer this back to horror for a moment, and ask ourselves this question: Are the characters in horror fiction different to the characters in general fiction?

Well, yes and no.

The major difference, perhaps, is that the characters in horror fiction are often confronted by the supernatural. This doesn't mean that the characters *themselves* are different, simply that the situations in which they find themselves often are. It also means that you, as the writer, have to work extra hard to portray an appropriate response to a situation for which there is no comparison in real life.

Imagination comes into play here, of course. But then imagination comes into play whether you're writing supernatural fiction, crime fiction or a novel about two people having an affair. But whereas the emotions and experiences associated with having an affair can be readily accessed from people who have had them, if not experienced directly, it's more difficult to find reliable firsthand accounts of people confronted by, say, vampires or demons.

It's important, though, to get such reactions as right as you possibly can. Nothing undermines a horror story more than unconvincing character responses to the often outrageous events they're faced with. For a good horror story to work it's important that it is grounded in reality as much as possible. If you honestly can't imagine how you, or your characters, might feel when confronted by a demon or a vampire, it could be that you're working in the wrong genre. Or it could just be that you need some kind of impetus, a jumping-off point – in which case, I would suggest seeking out firsthand accounts from people confronted by real-life horrors – a shark, a gunman, an approaching tsunami – and then try to take it one step further, to add an extra element of wonder, disbelief, a sense that the reality you believed in, that you relied on, has been undermined, swept away.

As well as writing about ordinary people confronted by the supernatural, it's also true to say that as horror writers you might sometimes find yourself creating characters who are more extreme, in terms of motivation or behaviour, than those ordinarily found in general fiction. You might choose, for example, to make your 'monster' the viewpoint character of your book, be that a supernatural creation, like the 200-year-old vampire Louis de Pointe du Lac in Anne Rice's *Interview With a Vampire*, or an all-too-human sociopath like Patrick Bateman in Bret Easton Ellis's *American Psycho*.

Let's end by focusing briefly on this latter character, and on how Ellis brings him to life. One of the most notorious modern-day 'monsters' to emerge from horror fiction, Patrick Bateman is a Wall Street investment banker and cold-hearted serial killer – or is he? Because, interestingly, there is an argument that Bateman may be what is often referred to as an 'unreliable narrator', in which case the brutal killings that he chronicles in such cold and clinical detail may simply be fantasies, figments of his imagination. At the final reckoning, it is entirely up to the reader to decide whether to believe Bateman's account of his activities or not – a dilemma, incidentally, which could, in truth, be applied to all books written in the first person.

Bateman's repellent and obsessive character is perhaps most readily expressed via his often excruciating attention to detail (his almost autistic labelling of brand names is blackly humorous). His chronicling of his morning routines – personal hygiene, fitness, diet – spans pages of dense, sometimes repetitive text and becomes almost like a mantra. His speech is characterised by language which parrots phrases and information he's read in press releases or product reviews. It is as if he's a cypher pretending to be a real person, and desperately trying to cover the fact that he isn't – a trick that, for a writer, is difficult to pull off, but which Ellis does with aplomb. The irony is that even when Bateman spouts gibberish to cover for the fact that he knows nothing about certain topics, his equally materialistic colleagues are so self-obsessed that they don't notice.

As well as being a meticulously rendered character in his own right, Bateman is also, of course, a symbol for the cold and corrupting nature of materialism, of excessive wealth. He hates minorities, gay males, the homeless, the poor, and to some extent women, almost as a matter of course. Whether real or imagined, his murders – of men, women, children and animals – are shocking not only because they're sickeningly brutal, but also because he relates them in such icy, matter-of-fact detail that his choice of language suggests he gets no real gratification from them, that inflicting pain and taking lives is just something he does to pass the time, the ultimate nihilistic statement.

Bateman is merely one extreme but frighteningly believable character among many to be found in horror fiction. Others – Jack Torrance in *The Shining*, Frank in *The Wasp Factory* – can be encountered in the reading list below. Most of the characters to be found in horror fiction, though, are just like you and me – ordinary people living ordinary lives until the extraordinary impinges upon them. It is important to remember that these people should form the solid foundations of your story, and that if you don't get them right, your ideas, no matter how good, will sink without trace.

EXERCISE

Come up with two characters, one male, one female. Write at least an A4 page of notes on each. Think about all the things, and more, that I talked about in my article. Think about when and where they were born, what their family backgrounds were like, who their friends are (or were), who they've had relationships with, what they do (or did) for a living. Think about their interests, their attitudes, their beliefs. Think about what *kind* of people they are – cautious or confident; diffident or loud-mouthed; resourceful or hapless; prejudiced or open-minded etc.

Let your imagination flow during this exercise. Jot down anything that occurs to you. Maybe one of them has a tattoo; maybe one of them once saved someone's life; maybe one has a debilitating illness that requires constant medication; maybe one has a dark secret.

Once you're confident that you know your two characters well enough, write a scene or a story (don't hamper your creativity by imposing a word limit) in which the two of them are stuck in a lift and forced to interact. What will happen? Will they bond? Argue? What role or outlook will each of them adopt?

If you've done the exercise properly, then the scene should flow; it should crackle with energy. You should find that there's so much information you *want* to include that writing the scene will become a process not of wondering what to write next, but of deciding what you can and should leave out.

TOP TIPS

- Write every day. If you're really serious about being a writer you'll find the time. It takes, on average, about half an hour to write a page of fiction. So even if you write only one page a day, by the end of the year you'll have 365 pages – a novel.

- Don't be put off by rejection. If your work gets rejected it doesn't mean it's rubbish. It means that in someone else's opinion, it wasn't, for whatever reason, quite right for them. To put this into perspective, I'm currently editing a story anthology with around twenty slots, for which (in the first three months of the five-month submission window) I've received over six hundred stories. This means I've had to turn away a large amount of very good, perfectly publishable work. So if one market *does* reject your story, just send it elsewhere.

- Be adaptable and fearless. Don't limit yourself by staying safely within your comfort zone. Don't automatically say no to projects you don't think you can handle. My policy is to say yes first, and worry about how I'm going to do it afterwards. Because of this attitude, I once agreed to write a novel in four weeks for Titan Books based on the Starz TV series *Spartacus*, even though I hadn't seen the series and knew nothing about ancient Rome. I watched the entire series in two days and researched what I needed to on the hoof. Although it was hard, often gruelling work, the novel turned out okay, and led to Titan offering me a three-book deal for my own fiction.

TEN EXCELLENT, CHARACTER-LED HORROR NOVELS TO SINK YOUR TEETH INTO

The Wasp Factory – Iain Banks
The Face That Must Die – Ramsey Campbell
American Psycho – Bret Easton Ellis
The Woodwitch – Stephen Gregory

The Tooth Fairy – Graham Joyce
The Shining – Stephen King
The Three – Sarah Lotz
The Ritual – Adam Nevill
The Language of Dying – Sarah Pinborough
Ghost Story – Peter Straub

ALISON MOORE

LIVING IN A REAL WORLD

ONE OF MY favourite quotes about writing is one James Thurber tells about himself: 'Sometimes my wife comes up to me at a party and says, "Damnit, Thurber, stop writing." She usually catches me in the middle of a paragraph. Or my daughter will look up from the dinner table and ask, "Is he sick?" "No," my wife says, "he's writing something."'

Writing is one way of living multiple lives, partly because writing my protagonists usually feels like I'm 'wearing' them and seeing through their eyes, and partly because if a story is working, its fictional environment becomes as real to me as any other place I've been to. I had a confused conversation with a lady who asked me where I'd got the idea for my novel, *The Lighthouse*. 'I saw a man,' I said, 'sitting at a kitchen table.' 'So he was a real person?' she said. 'Oh, no,' I said, but as I tried to explain seeing this image of a man sitting at a kitchen table, I still failed make him sound made-up and succeeded only in convincing the lady that I really had seen this man. I think the problem I was having was that he didn't feel like someone I'd conjured up with my imagination; it felt as if I were seeing him, watching him through 'the fourth wall'. For me, the most satisfying writing is when I'm only writing down what I can see (and even now I have to remember to add: *in my head*). It's wonderful to arrive at the point in a story – I experienced it again whilst working on my second novel – where you can, through your characters, walk up and down the streets of your fictional world; you can enter its buildings and approach its inhabitants; it's almost like lucid dreaming.

In that scene in which I first 'saw' the character who would become Futh, he was sitting at the kitchen table of a woman with whom he had once had a relationship. The woman was elsewhere in the house and didn't know he was there. And his shoes were hurting his feet. This scene, in the end, isn't in *The Lighthouse*, but it was a vital part of the novel's origination, revealing to me what the story was about, what its themes were. The spirit of this scene remains in the young Futh's spying on Gloria and subsequently inhabiting her kitchen, although, unlike in that original scene, he is invited in; and the woman's being elsewhere and barely aware of him remains in the guise of Futh's absent and indifferent mother. This was, I could see, a story about loss, returning and repetition. Futh is like the ghost ship his father talks about, 'crashing over and over again into the rocks around the lighthouse'. It is the story of a man who is having trouble finding his way. As soon as I put this character and these themes into the right setting – a circular walking holiday in another country – it gained movement and momentum, a life of its own.

The trip Futh takes – from Harwich to the Hook of Holland and then to Germany to walk along the Rhine – is one I'd taken a couple of years earlier, and I'd kept a diary, so I knew what Futh could see from the outer deck of the ferry and I knew what his cabin was like, although the storm he experiences was lifted from a later, cross-channel trip. Therein lies another benefit of being a writer: you can be, for example, grim with seasickness and at the same time be taking notes and thinking about how well this will fit into the story you're working on.

The first chapter (in which Futh is on a North Sea ferry, setting out on his adventure) told me how the final chapter needed to be, which in turn informed the penultimate chapter. Filling in the rest was as much of a journey for me as for Futh. While the Rhineland location was drawn from real life, from experience, Hellhaus itself is fictional. It helped that I really had walked through the same woods and over the same fields as Futh, but the made-up homes and hotels seemed equally real to me.

Having got a handle on Futh's story, I now understood the importance of the Hellhaus hotel at which he stays on both his first and last night in Germany, and so I interleaved his chapters with the story of what's developing there while he's on his week-long walk. Initially, Ester was a minor character, supporting Futh's story, but just as Futh was in charge of his chapters, leading the way (even if his instincts were poor and his choices ill-advised), so Ester began to take over more of her part of the narrative. She soon became an equal player, to the extent that some readers see *The Lighthouse* more as Ester's story than Futh's.

Sometimes I'll write a passage or a detail not knowing quite why it should be in the story, but if it feels right I go with it and sooner or later I'll understand how it fits in, why it belongs. The warnings scattered throughout the narrative came freely, as if the story's minor characters knew better than me where all this was heading and were trying to intervene. Before he reaches Hellhaus, they say to him, 'Stay away', or, 'Stay here'. At the hotel, it is Bernard who says to Futh, 'You should go', and to another man, 'Get the fuck out'. When Futh is walking away from Hellhaus, he is told that he is 'going in the right direction'. As he makes his way back, he is told, 'You want to be going in the other direction.' Very often, I only become aware of the story's undercurrent as I'm going along, and then I can go back and beef it up accordingly, adding, for instance, Futh's father's monologue about lighthouse warning systems and the details of the hazard signs on the ferry's car deck (which I only deliberately observed on that second ferry trip).

The first draft was half the length of the second but contained the essence of the story. On completing those first 25,000 words, I knew what I wanted to go back and add, working it up to 50,000 words. After that, though, I read the manuscript through many times, moving and tweaking things. I also read only Futh's chapters and then only Ester's chapters to reinforce my sense of their separate experiences and to make sure there were no incongruities there, checking that I did not have Futh falling asleep naked but waking up wearing pyjamas. I worked out which guests Ester has staying in which rooms on which nights, to make sure she was not cleaning rooms that had not been used. There is one scene – a memory of a family picnic in Cornwall – that is returned to a number of times, and each time we see or focus on slightly different details. By lifting out these passages and looking at them side by side, I could check for inconsistencies, making sure that the father packs away the picnic items and folds up the picnic blanket in the same order each time. Additionally, I had my two readers: my editor Nicholas Royle, who is excellent on factual accuracy and consistency, and my husband Dan. In an early draft of the first paragraph, I wrote that Futh 'has only been on a ferry once before, when he was twelve and going abroad for the first time with his father'. Dan pointed out that if he'd been there and back, he'd actually been on a ferry twice before. However many times and however carefully you read through your work, an extra pair of eyes never goes amiss. Amongst the things I've heard said about the difference between short stories and novels is that in a novel you can get away with a baggy paragraph. Personally, I'd be as mortified to discover a chunk of shabby writing hiding amongst the two hundred pages of my novel as I would to find one glaring out of a two-thousand-word story. I find myself approaching novel writing in very much the same way as I approach short story writing. I was revising the text pretty much up to the moment *The Lighthouse* went to press, although that still isn't to say there's been nothing to kick myself over since publication.

Of course the point of all this, the point of convincing myself of this world and of revising and revising to eliminate factual errors and inconsistencies is so that the reader will in turn be convinced of this world. Whether or not the reader will *like* it is a different matter. After a reading of *The Lighthouse* at a London library, I was tackled by one woman on one side of the room about why it was necessary for Bernard to have been so brutal, and by another woman on the opposite side of the room as to why Bernard would stay with a woman like Ester. Both of these readers seemed quietly furious, and while I endeavoured to give satisfactory answers to their questions, what really struck me was that they had sufficient belief in this fictional world to be severely offended by the behaviour and choices of the characters. They were taking me to task not over the quality of my writing but for bringing such people into being. Deep down, I rate this as a rather positive and encouraging reader response.

EXERCISE

This is an exercise that went down well at a recent workshop on 'landscape and setting'. The exercise is in two parts. Participants should complete the first part before knowing what the second part entails:

- You've been walking in the countryside, on the moors or on a coastal path, and now you're lost and it's getting late, the light's going. You see a house and the lights are on. You approach and knock on the door. Who answers? How are you received?
- Now write the scene from the point of view of whoever opened the door.

TOP TIPS

- When I was younger, I would sometimes get an idea for a story, jot it down and put it in a shoebox under my bed. That would be fine if they were just fermenting down there until the time was right but I don't think a single one of these ever came out and got written. This was like waiting for the water to run warm without having turned on the tap. I had to learn to get stuck in, explore these ideas and simply write more stories.
- It can seem as if life sometimes gets in the way of writing, but life is where the writing comes from. I'm rarely sitting in front of my computer when I find my stories – stories have come to me on family outings, in the pub, at work or walking to work or on the train, while getting quotes for a job on the house, and from the experience of being pregnant and having a baby.
- It took me a very long time to feel able to show my work to someone I knew, as opposed to just sending it out to a magazine or a competition. When I finally did, though, the feedback was really valuable. But make sure it's someone you trust, only show work when you're ready to, and re-member feedback is subjective, you can disagree.

TEN EXCELLENT NOVELS

Graham Greene, *Brighton Rock*
Patricia Highsmith, *The Talented Mr Ripley*
Shirley Jackson, *We Have Always Lived in the Castle*
Stephen King, *Misery*
Ian McEwan, *The Comfort of Strangers*
George Orwell, *Keep the Aspidistra Flying*
Muriel Spark, *The Driver's Seat*
John Steinbeck, *Of Mice and Men*
Kurt Vonnegut, *Slaughterhouse-Five*
Richard Yates, *Disturbing the Peace*

NICHOLAS ROYLE

THE DEATH OF THE AUTHOR

T HIS PHRASE HAS the frisson of a Roland Barthes © or
even ™. His 1968 essay of this title is widely viewed as
encapsulating the spirit of 'French theory' and is by now, as
they say, a classic. 'The Death of the Author' is vibrant, witty,
profound, provocative, flamboyant and uneven. In his long-
unfashionable but also brilliant *Aspects of the Novel* (1927),
EM Forster remarks on 'what is always provocative in a work
of art: roughness of surface' (124). He is talking about novels that are 'full of dents and grooves and lumps and spikes
which draw from us little cries of approval and disapproval',
but 'when they have passed the roughness is forgotten, they
become as smooth as the moon' (124-5). If this is character-
istic of the novels of Dostoevsky, Melville, DH Lawrence and
Emily Brontë, as Forster suggests, perhaps something similar
applies to the art of essay-writing. *Roughness* might seem an
odd word to use of Barthes's writing, for it is invariably elegant
and discriminating. Unable to conceal its love of words, his
prose is at once poetic and readable. It has great deftness and
sensitivity. Still there is a roughness, even if it is a loving roughness, in the way that Barthes collects, pushes together and

juxtaposes different ideas and arguments that are, in 1968, 'of the moment' on the French intellectual and political scene. As a result, his essay gives a very good *rough* sense of what people are talking about when they talk about 'structuralism', 'post-structuralism' and 'postmodernism', even if it happily contains none of those ugly words themselves.

The roughness starts with the title. Barthes announces the *death* of the author, and in the essay itself 'the destruction' and 'the removal of the Author' (145), but he knows things are not so simple. He is not speaking literally, reporting on some global phenomenon of authors being killed. Nor is he advocating that authors be put to death. There is an irreducible element of paradox in the capital 'A' he gives to his subject. Barthes is an exuberantly ludic writer. As Jonathan Culler has summarily noted, 'his writing is too playful to authorise a definite conclusion' (16). Still, 'The Death of the Author' has valuable, even life-changingly important things to say. Barthes gathers together strands of critical thinking from philosophy, history, linguistics, psychoanalysis, Marxism, religion, anthropology and literature itself. All of these enable him to argue that a sort of revolution is going on in terms of how we think about the figure of the author, authorship and authority.

If you were ever at all inclined to think of the author as a kind of God-like figure (that is exactly what the word 'Author' re-fers to, for example, in Milton's *Paradise Lost*), or to think of the author as the source or presiding authority of the text (the words 'author' and 'authority' share a history: they go back down the centuries, hand in hand, into the world of Latin), or to think of novels or poems primarily (or even a little bit) as works in which the author *expresses* herself or himself – well, forget it. It's time to wake up and reckon with what various poetic and critical thinkers have been saying for decades. It's time to acknowledge that, in fundamental respects, 'it is language which speaks, not the author' (143). It's time to accept that the meaning or, more generally, a critical reading of a novel or poem cannot be limited to what we think the author meant or, even worse, what an author *says* she meant.

Language gets up to stuff without our say-so. Grammar, vocabulary, syntax – all constrain what we can say. Language was there before us and it will be there to see us off. No one owns it. We can calculate and try to control things, but there is always chance and the unforeseeable. There are always unconscious or inadvertent effects. (A perhaps familiar scenario when you hear an author talking about his work: 'I didn't mean it to sound like *that!*' or 'Thank you! I hadn't actually made that connection myself', and so on.) Even or perhaps especially in extreme cases, such as Stéphane Mallarmé's *Un Coup de Dés* (1897) or James Joyce's *Finnegans Wake* (1940), language takes on a life of its own. Thus Barthes declares with a seductive flourish:

> We know now that a text is not a line of words releasing a single 'theological' meaning (the 'message' of the Author-God) but a multi-dimensional space in which a variety of writings, none of them original, blend and clash. The text is a tissue of quotations drawn from the innumerable centres of culture. (146)

Now we know. 'The Death of the Author' is a powerful polemic, directed with particular cogency against those for whom 'the *explanation* of a work is always [to be] sought in the man or woman who produced it' (143).

The essay concludes on a less persuasive note. It makes a rough landing, as it were, as Barthes shifts from a putdown of the author to a misleading privileging of the *reader*. In his final words he asserts: 'the birth of the reader must be at the cost of the death of the Author' (148). The trouble with this is that much of what he has argued earlier in the essay about the figure of the *author* must also apply to that of the *reader*. He might better (though less flamboyantly) have rested his case with a claim for the birth of a new kind of *reading*, and avoided the rather troubling, sacrificial image of reader and author as Siamese twins. Nonetheless, here and in other writings, Barthes's focus on the reader proved influential – especially in the fields of reader-response criticism, narrative theory and narratology. His meticulous and inventive encounters with Balzac's *Sarrasine* (in *S/Z*) or Poe (in 'Textual Analysis of Poe's "Valdemar"') are wonderful examples of how to read and where it might take you, of the pleasures and treasures of reading fiction.

Barthes returns to the idea of the death or removal or papering-over of the author in a rather less delirious, more systematic essay, 'From Work to Text' (1971). Here he observes:

> If the author is a novelist, he is inscribed in the novel like one of his characters, figured in the carpet; no longer privileged and paternal, the locus of genuine truth, his inscription is ludic. He becomes, as it were, a 'paper-author': his life is no longer the origin of his fictions, but a fiction contributing to his work . . . The *I* that writes the text is never, itself, anything more than a paper-*I*. (161, trans. mod.)

There are at least two intertwining elements of uncomfortable truth in this, namely:

(1) You want to write about yourself in the first person, either in a fictional or in a more conventionally autobiographical fashion, and you quickly come to perceive how this written 'I' seems to develop its own identity and differ, however subtly or radically, from what you had planned or imagined. It may be disconcerting, frustrating, disorienting that this 'I' is not the 'I' you hoped or envisaged, or the 'I' the 'I' thought it was. (It is no wonder that philosophers, from Plato to Derrida, talk of the text as a child, writing as an orphan, and so on.) But it can also be pleasurable. This is a source of the sort of playfulness associated with metafiction (John Barth, Muriel Spark, Philip Roth), with novelists writing novels about novelists writing novels . . . But as quickly becomes evident, there is also something mechanical and deadly about all this. In this context we may recall the eerie glue that holds together the narrator of Margaret Atwood's story 'Giving Birth' (1977): 'These are the only words I have, I'm stuck with them, stuck in them' (225-6).

(2) And at the same time, you *are going to die*. It might be later today or many years from now, but sooner or later you will be wormfood or go up in smoke or something similarly unthinkable, and the only 'I' that will be left will be the 'I' of your writing. This is the darker, more literal 'death of the author' that Barthes's essay, intriguingly, leaves unspoken. Such is the figure glossed by Jacques Derrida when he observes that the author is 'dead insofar as his text has a structure of survival even if he is living' ('Des Tours de Babel', 183). Derrida's point is that a novel is composed of writing and that this writing, at least potentially or in principle, lasts longer than the author. The capacity for a piece of writing to survive

means that, in a significant if spooky way, the author is in effect already dead. Novel-writing is necessarily a ghostly business.

In recent years there has been a wide-scale reaction against 'theory' (French or otherwise) and a tendency to see the apocalyptic 'death of the author' proclaimed by Barthes as marking what Seán Burke calls the 'melancholy retreat' of academic literary criticism into a world of self-enclosing jargon, away from the politics of '"real life"' (ix). (The scare quotes around 'real life' are Burke's, and their necessity is just the sort of thing that Barthes's work lucidly exposes and analyses.) The past couple of decades in particular have witnessed a sort of attempted restoration of the author. He has undergone major surgery but been patched up and now look – just like new! But such restorative or reconstructive work is shoddy and disingenuous. It involves a desire to disavow, to play down or deny powerful truths. More perniciously, it also seems to be bound up with the insidious workings of the marketplace. Two notable manifestations of this restoration may be seen in the continuing growth of 'creative writing' (in schools and universities, and elsewhere) and in the emergence of what is called 'life writing'. The (increasingly marketised) academy is alive and well. 'Creative writing' and 'life writing', after all, sound decidedly life-giving, life-affirming, vital. Nothing deadly going on here. Death of the author? Who's talking about the death of the author?

It's a funny old phrase, 'the death of the author'. If you brush away the metaphorical dust, these words can appear in various respects strange, even (dare I say) uncanny. What is this repetition of 'the' about? It might, paradoxically, help to remind us of the significance of singularity – the fact that every author is different, every novel is singular, and also every death. No one else can die your death for you. And at the same time you have no 'real' relationship to that death. 'Real life', 'real death'. 'Death' is always the name of a secret. The repeated 'the' perhaps stammers something of this. As Freud recognised, 'it is indeed impossible to imagine our own death; and whenever we do so we can perceive that we are in fact still present as spectators' ('Thoughts for the Times', 77). If these things were not the case, what would be the point of novels? Perhaps better than any other kind of writing, novels can approach, evoke and explore the strangeness of death. And every novelist will go about this differently. The 'death' of JK Rowling is not the 'death' of Roberto Bolaño. As Frank Kermode's *The Sense of an Ending* (1967) suggests, every novel has its own singular way of ending, every novelist his or her own singular way of bringing the life or the world of a novel to its end. The peculiarity of the work of fiction has to do with the fact that its end is foreseen by its author. If only in principle, the author is a figure endowed with second-sight. Not only is the end known in advance, but everything before it paves the way toward that end. Hence the continuing richness and interest of Peter Brooks's *Reading for the Plot* (1984), which reads Freud's *Beyond the Pleasure Principle* as a kind of bizarre theory of narrative suggesting that every fictional plot is haunted by 'the danger of reaching the end too quickly, of achieving the im-proper death' or 'improper end' (104). To adapt Freud's phrasing in *Beyond the Pleasure Principle*, every novel 'wishes to die only in its own fashion' (312). We are not far here, perhaps, from Walter Benjamin's lapidary remark in 'The Storyteller' (1936): 'Death is the sanction of everything that the storyteller can tell. He has borrowed his authority from death' (94).

In 'What Is an Author?' (1969), Michel Foucault makes the

point that 'the author's name is not . . . just a proper name like the rest' (146). He goes on:

> It would seem that the author's name, unlike other proper names, does not pass from the interior of a discourse to the real and exterior individual who produced it; instead, the name seems always to be present, marking off the edges of the text, revealing, or at least characterising, its mode of being. (147)

Again, there is something ghostly intimated here. When it comes to the art of the novel, the name 'Virginia Woolf' or 'Don DeLillo', for example, is not something that simply stands outside the text, but rather marks the interior, haunts its edges. This has to do with what Raymond Carver calls 'the writer's particular and unmistakable signature on everything he writes' (22). You can read a paragraph by Woolf and it seems to have 'Woolf' written across it in invisible ink. You read a sentence or two of DeLillo and it's recognisably the work of DeLillo. In a remarkable essay entitled *Signsponge* (originally published in 1975), Derrida investigates such workings of the proper name, the signature and authorial desire. In doing so he makes pointed reference to 'that death or omission of the author of which, as is certainly the case, too much of a case has been made' (22). At any event, it would seem that 'what is an author?' very much remains, as the saying goes, a live question. Which is not to suggest that we know what 'live' means here, or that we should put aside the insights and excitement of reading Barthes, Foucault or Derrida. It is also worth noting that *Signsponge* is perhaps the most profound critical meditation ever written about the ways in which a novelist or poet is *always* engaged in a deadly duel (think *Moby-Dick*), and the author's desire to sign his or her work ineluctably entails an encounter with 'something entirely other' – 'death, in short' (48).

Even (dare I say) uncanny, I said. What is an author to do if his name is Nicholas Royle and someone else called Nicholas Royle asks him to write an essay entitled 'The Death of the Author'? How will the reader know if there really are two of them, in 'real life', particularly given they both seem to share a preoccupation with the uncanny, which is manifested in all sorts of ways, deliberately or not, in everything they write? Even or perhaps especially after their deaths it may prove impossible to tell these authors apart. They are, as one of them suggests in an essay about the uncanniness of the double, 'mortgaged beyond the hilt' (191). I haven't the faintest idea what he would say, if he were to write a short text called 'The Death of the Author'. I imagine the task might drive him mad. But I suspect that at least some readers will believe he wrote these pages.

REFERENCES

Atwood, Margaret. 'Giving Birth'. In *Dancing Girls and Other Stories*. London: Virago, 1985.
Barthes, Roland. 'The Death of the Author' and 'From Work to Text'. In *Image Music Text*, trans. Stephen Heath. London: Fontana, 1977.
Barthes, Roland. *S/Z*, trans. Richard Miller. London: Jonathan Cape, 1975.
Barthes, Roland. 'Textual Analysis of Poe's "Valdemar"', trans. Geoff Bennington. In *Untying the Text: A Post-Structuralist Reader*, ed. Robert Young. London: Routledge and Kegan Paul, 1981.
Benjamin, Walter. 'The Storyteller', trans. Harry Zohn. In

Illuminations: Essays and Reflections, ed. Hannah Arendt. New York: Schocken Books, 1969.

Brooks, Peter. *Reading for the Plot: Design and Intention in Narrative*. Cambridge, Mass.: Harvard University Press, 1984.

Burke, Seán. *The Death and Return of the Author: Criticism and Subjectivity in Barthes, Foucault and Derrida*. 2nd edition. Edinburgh: Edinburgh University Press, 1998.

Carver, Raymond. 'On Writing'. In *Fires: Essays, Poems, Stories*. London: Picador, 1986.

Culler, Jonathan. *Roland Barthes*. London: Fontana, 1983.

Derrida, Jacques. *Signéponge/Signsponge*, trans. Richard Rand. New York: Columbia University Press, 1984.

Derrida, Jacques. 'Des Tours de Babel', trans. Joseph F. Grahame. In *Difference in Translation*, ed. Joseph F. Graham. Ithaca: Cornell University Press, 1985.

Forster, EM *Aspects of the Novel*, ed. Oliver Stallybrass. Harmondsworth: Penguin, 1976.

Foucault, Michel. 'What is an Author?', trans. Josue V Harari. In *Textual Strategies: Perspectives in Post-Structuralist Criticism*, ed. Josue V Harari. London: Methuen, 1980.

Freud, Sigmund. *Beyond the Pleasure Principle*. In *Pelican Freud Library*, vol. 11, trans. James Strachey. Harmondsworth: Penguin, 1984.

Freud, Sigmund. 'Thoughts for the Times on War and Death'. In *Pelican Freud Library*, vol. 12, trans. James Strachey. Harmondsworth: Penguin,1985.

Kermode, Frank. *The Sense of an Ending: Studies in the Theory of Fiction*. Oxford: Oxford University Press, 1967.

Royle, Nicholas. 'The Double'. In *The Uncanny*. Manchester: Manchester University Press, 2003.

EXERCISE

Basil Bunting once remarked that it is easier to die than to remember. There is an amazing little book by Joe Brainard, called *I Remember*, which simply consists of hundreds of sentences or short paragraphs that start 'I remember . . .' Write twenty sentences or short paragraphs on this model. (One or more, with luck, will be the basis for a piece of fiction.)

TOP TIPS

- Write every day. If there is a day or days when you can't, make sure you read or take notes about something that advances your writing project.
- Get a draft of the whole thing finished, no matter how execrable, insufficient and intolerable you may feel it to be.
- Whatever happens, avoid the temptation to be 'creative'. 'Creative' in the context of 'creative writing' usually means *deadly*.

TEN NOVELS THAT MIGHT TRANSFORM YOUR THINKING ABOUT FATE AND JUSTICE

Samuel Beckett, *The Unnamable*
Elizabeth Bowen, *The Death of the Heart*
Emily Brontë, *Wuthering Heights*
George Douglas Brown, *The House With the Green Shutters*
George Eliot, *Daniel Deronda*
Ralph Ellison, *Invisible Man*
William Faulkner, *Absalom, Absalom!*
Knut Hamsun, *Hunger*
James Hogg, *Confessions of a Justified Sinner*
Herman Melville, *Billy Budd*

ALICE THOMPSON

SURREALISM AND THE NOVEL

SURREALISM IS AS tricky and as slippery to describe as a melting clock, but my favourite writers – the ones who most pervasively influenced my own fiction – could all be called surrealist. So how to circumscribe surrealism when its very *raison d'être* is to defy categorisation?

Dreamscape is central to surrealism, where the Freudian idea of 'free association' liberates a reader from social conventions and traditional concepts. In surrealist writing connections are rewired, startling juxtapositions posited, and contrasting images inform the landscape. Surrealism shocks in its attempt to join the world of dream with an everday rational world, in, as André Breton wrote, an 'absolute reality, a surreality'.

Novelists such as Murakami, Pynchon and Calvino (postmodernism nicked surrealism's pyjamas) all toy with mixing reality with the outlandish in the most astute, matter-of-fact ways. This seems to me symptomatic of surrealist writing – its utter acceptance of the strange. For do we not in our dreams embrace everything on equal terms? In my novel *The*

Existential Detective[1], what is real and what is not become indeterminate, as Will struggles to find the solution to the ultimate puzzle – what is the nature of reality? – and fails. Paul Auster in *The New York Trilogy* also uses the detective genre to explore ontological questions. The dreamscape of surrealism seems to me to be just another way of asking what is real.

Another predicate of surrealism is poetic technique. Imagery, metaphor, allegory and onomatopoeia are all fundamental to the surrealist writer. Images rather than explanation form the carapace of such fiction. Kafka's cockroach in *Metamorphosis* or Muriel Spark's hallucinatory passages in *The Mandelbaum Gate* have multi-dimensional resonances that work psychically, politically and emotionally all at once. That is the beauty of them.

And there is a beauty to the surprising image that is not only erotic but subversive. Angela Carter writes in her essay 'The Alchemy of Words', 'Surrealist beauty is convulsive. That is, you feel it, you don't see it – it exists as an excitation of the nerves. The experience of the beautiful is, like the experience of desire, an abandonment to vertigo, yet the beautiful does not exist as such. What do exist are images or objects that are enigmatic, marvellously erotic – or juxtapositions of objects, or people, or ideas, that arbitrarily extend our notion of the connections it is possible to make. In a way, the beautiful is put at the service of liberty.'

These uncanny juxtapositions – such as made manifest in the cut-up technique of William Borroughs – make for complexity. Over-simplistic representations of life can be unsatisfactory and limiting and factually inaccurate. Dali writes, 'You

---

1 Please see Nicholas Royle's review of *The Existential Detective* in the *Independent* (14/7/2010) for an overview of the surrealist paintings depicted on my book covers. http://www.independent.co.uk/arts-entertainment/books/reviews/the-existential-detective-by-alice-thompson-2025765.html

have to systematically create confusion, it sets creativity free. Everything that is contradictory creates life.' There is dynamic energy to the unlikely juxtaposition or vivid image, which surrealism frequently offers and realism cannot.

Surrealism, and its association with dreaming, tends towards the symbolic. In *Lord of the Flies*, William Golding uses the image of a pig's head to symbolise a collapsing civilisation, and, in *The Spire*, he uses the image of a church spire to symbolise the dangers of religious fundamentalism. In my novel *Pharos*, the central symbol of the lighthouse uses the imagery of light and dark to explore religion, slavery and literal (as well as moral) blindness. In another of my novels, *Burnt Island*, the destruction of the doppelgängers of Max's family symbolises the end of his family life. It also suggests the ultimate destructive/cathartic nature of divorce and psychic change. Finally in this brief analysis of symbolism in my own fiction, in *Pandora's Box*, gender is constantly fluid – characters change sex, and the plastic surgeon Noah's construction of a perfect woman is seen as fundamentally unstable.

In her essay, Angela Carter explores gender and surrealism in a similarly ambiguous way, seeing surrealism's advocates as male-centric in their definitions of femininity before finally appropriating surrealism for herself: ' . . . although I thought [the surrealists] were wonderful, I had to give them up in the end. They were, with a few patronised exceptions, all men and they told me that I was the source of all mystery, beauty, and otherness, because I was a woman – and I knew that was not true. I knew I wanted my fair share of the imagination, too. Not an excessive amount, mind; I wasn't greedy. Just an equal share in the right to vision.'

In theory, surrealist writing eschews plot altogether – how wrong this is. Surrealists are besotted by plot, just not in the normal way. The prototype of surrealism is the seemingly anarchic *Alice in Wonderland*. Surrealists prefer a plot that takes flying leaps over chasms, that defies conventional logic but most importantly of all – like dreams again – has a plot that makes absolute sense on its own terms. *The Crying of Lot 49* could be argued to have far too much plot.

Thus, surrealism puts language to the forefront, with its emphasis on a poetical grammar, and its attraction to non-linear time rather than a straightforward trajectory of time and story.

André Breton's *Manifesto of Surrealism* was his way of dealing with the 'horrors of World War I'. Breton trained in psychiatry and medicine. He worked in a neurological hospital where he used Freud's psycholanalytical theories to treat soldiers suffering from shellshock. During the rise of Nazism and Fascism many surrealists were forced to flee to America; as World War II was about to begin, the surrealists' writings had become dangerously subversive.

Surrealism works well as an anarchic and also a dark force. In my novel *The Falconer*, the image of the falconer and his manipulation of his birds is meant to encapsulate the manipulative quality of Nazi ideology. The mythical beast in the petrified forest symbolises man's instinctive savagery. Myth and politics interconnect. There is an existential darkness to Muriel Spark that should not be underestimated. In *The Driver's Seat* a woman writes the script for her own murder. In *Memento Mori* people are told they are going to die in anonymous phone calls. Martin Stannard, Spark's biographer, discusses the influence of Mary Shelley on his subject, calling Shelley 'the originator of a kind of female gothic surrealism of which Muriel herself was to become the high priestess'. As I am very interested in the gothic, too, I find this equation between the gothic and surrealism fascinating.

There is a fine line between surrealism and the imagination

itself. They seem unequivocally connected. Surrealism is just the imagination unfettered. The unconscious, where dreams are made, is also the locus of the imagination. The less tethered to reality you are, the more surreal your imagination will be.

The central theme of all my books has been an exploration of what is real and what is not. How our subjective perception can read or even influence objective truth. How our hold on reality is by the very nature of our consciousness tenuous. Surrealism is the happy playground for this reading of an indeterminate world.

Surrealism is above all a form of writing that makes the reader think. It does not offer explanations lightly. It withholds and teases. The truth needs to be deciphered, like any cordoned-off murder scene. The reader is affected by surrealist writing in ways they may not understand at first. There are few, if any, explanations of what the story is *about*. Surrealism hands ultimate responsibility to the reader, saying, I trust you to endure a state of uncertainty, suggestiveness, an uneasy eroticism and a certain difficulty, in the name of a difficult pleasure.

In the first draft, I write intuitively, instinctually, without preplanning or maps. I have no idea where I am going, how I am going to get there or what I will find at the end. Rigorous logic and analysis may be needed in the following drafts but not during that first impulsive stage of writing. Surrealism favours the brave.

EXERCISE

Write a description of a place – either rural or urban – that you know. Rewrite it according to a specific state of mind or mood.

TOP TIPS

- 'One of the first things you learn as a writer is that you write what you can, not what you want.' Gabriel Garcia Marquez
- 'Style is the moment of identity between the writer and his subject.' Marcel Proust
- 'God keep me from ever completing anything. This whole book is but a draft – nay, but the draft of a draft. Oh, Time, Strength, Cash, and Patience!' Herman Melville

TEN SURREALIST NOVELS

Moby-Dick Herman Melville
Wuthering Heights Emily Brontë
The Golden Bowl Henry James
The Mandelbaum Gate Muriel Spark
To the Lighthouse Virginia Woolf
The Magic Toyshop Angela Carter
The Sea, the Sea Iris Murdoch
The Savage Detectives Roberto Bolaño
The Wind-up Bird Chronicle Haruki Murakami
The Crying of Lot 49 Thomas Pynchon

KERRY HUDSON

DETAILS, DETAILS . . .

A RE YOU SITTING comfortably? Yes? OK, I want you to
imagine a man and a woman in a room together. They're
having dinner. They have a small argument about something
but somehow they come to a resolution and then they sit smiling at each other.

How was it for you? Not so good? OK, let me try again...

Here are Dave and Alena in a small room in London. He's
tired after a long day at work. They begin to eat dinner. Alena
has cooked it specially to celebrate the fact she's just got a new
job. At first Dave misunderstands what the job is, so doesn't
show the proper amount of enthusiasm, and Alena gets upset.
Eventually they overcome their misunderstanding, ignore their
dinners getting cold and sit smiling at each other.

Better? Still disappointing somehow? Right, what about
this . . .

Dave comes home after a long, hard day. He's wearing the
cheap, shiny synthetic suit of a security guard. Alena, who
wears a rumpled too-big summer dress with the straps tied
at the shoulders, sits by his side on the sofa and watches him
as he unlaces his heavy boots, rolls his socks down over his

heels. She's cooked a special dinner, her movements have an excitable jerk to them as she brings the plates of grilled fish, the little eggcups filled with Russian salad to the table. The room is tiny and bare, a kitchenette counter along one wall, dirty woodchip wallpaper with the sheen of grease, a sofa, a TV. The windows are open letting in the sounds of a busy London street, sirens and raised voices, cars and buses, along with the orange-tinted summer dusk, the smell of dirt rising from city pavements. They sit side by side on the sofa, still not quite touching, eating the food from the plates on their laps. She tells him the news about her new job but he's distracted, misunderstands and so becomes frustrated with her. She gets upset, her features pinched trying to hold in tears. She compares herself unfavourably to the women he works with. He goes to comfort her, touch her, and then hesitates. He tells her he thinks she's amazing, that those girls can't hold a candle to her. Suddenly her temper is gone. She's smiling tearfully, leaning back against the sofa and he leans back beside her, their heads turned to meet each other's gaze. They sit like that, looking at each other, close but still not touching, the heat of the plates of food on their legs, the city spilling in through the open window.

Better? I think so. And while this is still not quite right – after all, we don't know who Dave and Alena are or why we should care for them, what the importance of her job is and we haven't heard any of their conversation – this version is still so much more satisfying.

So what is wrong with version one? Simply, there is nothing for the reader's imagination to grip upon. If writing and reading are largely collaborative acts (and I believe they very much are) then in this first version I was saying 'please do all the work for me. Here, I've given you scaffolding, please lay the foundations, erect the walls, install windows . . .'

The second version is a little better. To continue the 'house' analogy, it has foundations, windows and walls and yet I'm still asking you to conjure nearly a whole world, to make giant leaps of imagination and interpretation. I've given you an empty, bare house. Serviceable, but nowhere you'd want to spend time without doing some serious work of your own.

The third version, while still lacking many aspects of a complete story, is fuller, richer. This place has walls and windows, fitting and fixtures and, of course, you, the reader, will arrive and add your own personal touches based on who you are and how you perceive the world but I have already shaped the environment you'll bring that personal taste and perspective to. I have done most of the work and you will occupy that fictional space and interpret it.

Such is the importance of detail. I talk about 'detail' in fiction often . . . clues to aid discoveries, seeds that grow ideas about a certain character or place or situations, underpinning stitches, small anchors to root a piece of fiction in a feeling of 'truth'. I stand by all of these definitions. I believe good detail does all of these things and it is absolutely essential to elevating your writing.

Where are you reading this, I wonder? Are you at home in bed, under the duvet with a Siamese cat biting at your toes for attention. Are you on a bus? The windows steamed up as everyone crowds on to get home for work, bulging shopping bags hanging from the crooks of their elbows? Perhaps you're in a cafe, with the chink-chink-chink of cutlery on china, the low thrum of conversation, the entwined smells of food in the air? Wherever you are, in a minute I want you to put down this book and just stop. Sit for a moment – if you can be still you will focus better – and collect the details of the environment you are in. It doesn't matter if it's the bed you've slept in for twenty years or a cafe you ran into because it was starting to rain, there will be details you've never consciously observed before.

Now, break apart the present moment. Make note of how everything feels, physically. What sounds can you hear (there are always sounds even when you think there is silence)? What can you smell (likewise)? Now, go deeper, try to notice tiny, minute details. Do this as though at some point in the future your life and the lives of those you love will one day depend upon your being able to recount this moment of time in all its sensory and visual fullness.

OK, go do that, then come back.

Hello again. What did you notice, I wonder? Did you see an old toenail clipping curled in the bedroom carpet fibres. Did you notice how the women on either side of you in the the cafe have the same style and colour of trainers, both their legs crossed towards you like they are bracketing you in? Were you able to smell the menthol cherry scent of the breath of the old man sitting on the bus next to you? Hear the barely perceptible clicking sound as he rotates the sliver of sweetie in his mouth and it hits his false teeth?

The beauty of creativity, of writing, is that I could put twenty people in exactly the same environment at the same moment and what they discern, the details they observe, would be entirely different. The details we gather from our everyday lives are naturally shaped by our identities, our pasts, our fears and hopes.

From those few minutes of stillness, of presence in the moment, you have collected a sort of 'mental scrapbook' of details. Details that are likely unique to you, that can be appropriated for a character or woven through your fiction if you decide they will reveal something about the story, the character, will bring some colour to a narrative that feels like a cavernous half-finished house.

You can do this at any time, this 'gathering'. Even on the days you feel you don't have a single moment to write you can still be keenly observant, live in the present, collect a scrapbook of ideas to use when you do have time to write. There is the myth of writers being entirely interior but I believe that we must be present and alert in our current world in order to find stories, to be able to give our reader the necessary seeds, anchors, clues to meet us halfway on our story's path and walk with us to The End.

There is a beautiful passage in Ruth Ozeki's *A Tale for the Time Being* where she references an ancient Buddhist text in which a Zen Master talks about the 6,400,099,980 'moments' that make up a single day. His point is that at any moment we can use a moment to change the course of things, to be better people. I like to think that in any single one of those 6,400,099,980 moments we can notice a detail which can bring life to our writing. And this is a practice, like meditation or running or, indeed, the act of writing itself, and is something which is learned and strengthened in time. A positive habit to be developed so that you will instinctively become more observant. I would go as far as to say that this practice won't just make your writing more alive, more 'real', but that it will make each day a little richer, simply because you are doing something that will greatly improve your ability to tell a story, and it will bring all of the great pleasure of that, too.

EXERCISE

Take a notebook to somewhere where there is lots of activity, lots of 'foot traffic' (I used to do this on Kingsland Road in London or at my local leisure centre cafe during the chaotic Saturday afternoon rush). Now sit for thirty minutes and write down as many details as you possibly can in that time. By the end you should have a few pages of unrelated details. For instance, the first few items from my Kingsland Road list would would read: light-up trainers, garish plastic roses dirty in the gutter, the smell of someone's coffee, a wheely trolley with a teddy bear sticking out, Elvis blasting through a car window etc.

Now your challenge is to weave each and every detail on this list through a new or current work of fiction. This will force you to build connections that aren't necessarily there, look at how your character(s) might interact with that specific detail, what that detail might reveal about your intention for the piece. Of course, you can then take out all of the details once you've done this exercise, but it's likely you'll find one or two which improve your piece or that the temporary inclusion of something you do eventually decide to take out has 'tilted' your story in a way you never anticipated.

TOP TIPS

- Get your arse on the seat: writers write.
- Write your 'shitty first draft' solely for yourself. Edit and revise for your readers.
- Be kind, work hard, don't be an arsehole.

TEN NOVELS WITH BEATING HEARTS AT THEIR CENTRE

Jack Kerouac, *On the Road*
Janice Galloway, *This is Not About Me*
Roddy Doyle, *The Barrytown Trilogy*
George Orwell, *The Road to Wigan Pier*
Carson McCullers, *The Heart is a Lonely Hunter*
Joyce Carol Oates, *Middle Age: A Romance*

AM Homes, *Music For Torching*
Sylvia Plath, *The Bell Jar*
JD Salinger, *The Catcher in the Rye*
Harper Lee, *To Kill a Mockingbird*

TOBY LITT

HOW TO MAKE THINGS DIFFICULT FOR YOURSELF: AN A–Z

Advice is in italics.
Sarcastic advice is in bold italics.

ANCESTORS

All writers, even semi-literate ones, have them – those prede-
cessors, grandfathers and great-grandmothers, who once upon
a time made a tone or technique or subject area possible.

Your ancestors may already be in plain view or may remain
forever invisible to you. The important thing is to venerate
them enough so the power of their distinctiveness (also known
as their *might*) doesn't destroy you, but also to find ways of
sneaking round behind them, of existing in their shadow, of
undermining their foundations.

Some writers' entire trajectory is to escape another writer.
Beckett was, most of all, not-Joyce.

I have discovered that the easiest way for me to stop writing is intensively to read certain of my ancestors. I will name only a few of the most terrifying. These are The Great Shutter-Uppers: Franz Kafka, James Joyce, Samuel Beckett. These are the writers I wish I could be – or I wish I had been. You'll see they are all male, all self-torturing. They are also (as I know to my cost) not worth imitating. They can be learned from but not closely approached.

Facing off against them, high on the opposite wall of the temple, are The Great Openers-Out: Walt Whitman, DH Lawrence, Virginia Woolf. These are writers who make my own writing seem more possible. I don't wish to *be* them – I wish to pass through some of the doors they opened. Doors of generosity, passion, perception, sentence structure. And so I say praises to my ancestors.

Although you may not be able to choose your own Ancestors, you can choose when and how to approach them – during which festivals, with which gifts. In other words, you can read them pragmatically or self-destructively. I have found that Whitman is the most generous of all Ancestors.

Immerse yourself for hours in your most fearsome Ancestor, then turn immediately to your own page.

Further Reading: Harold Bloom, *The Anxiety of Influence*, Oxford University Press.

BEGINNINGS

Extreme beginnings make for extreme difficulties. (See **Prose**.) The easiest solution is to stop making beginnings.

By far the hardest part of any fiction writing is the middle, particularly the second half of the middle – when all the introducing has been done and none of the climaxing has begun. Beginnings, contrastingly and illusorily, seem wonderfully free and easy.

Beginnings are when writers are at their most vain; when they think extreme success might be possible.

As a writer, you need the intelligence to begin and the stupidity to finish.

Get past the beginning as soon as you can. Acknowledge that, with the first full stop, ends the honeymoon period. If you can't deal with the grind of the middle, fuck off back to telling your friends and family how much you really want to write.

Make nothing but beginnings. Never get to the second half of the middle of anything. Dwell always in the honeymoon suite.

Further Reading: There will only Further Reading when it seems essential.

CAPITALISM

It's where we live, and we have no choice in the matter – unless we collectively choose to change it. If you remove the unnecessary 'American' from the following sentence, Jonathan Franzen speaks truly: 'The American writer today faces a cultural totalitarianism analogous to the political totalitarianism with which two generations of Eastern bloc writers had to contend. To ignore it is to court nostalgia. To engage with it, however, is to risk writing fiction that makes the same point over and over: technological consumerism is an infernal machine, technological consumerism is an infernal machine . . .' (See **Satire** and **United States.**)

Finding a way to afford to be a writer without selling out is hard.

Believe that you will never be able to write your work unless you do it on the latest computer, using the best software. Purchase apps. Take part in NaNoWriMo, annually. Go onto discussion forums and try to second-guess what gets certain editors at certain publishers hot. Self-publicise furiously. If there's a game, play it.

Further Reading: Jonathan Franzen, 'Why Bother: The *Harper's* Essay' in *How To Be Alone*, Fourth Estate, 2002.

DEATH

Cuts both ways. You can either think, 'I am going to die and all human endeavour will ultimately fail, therefore why write?' Or you can think, 'I am going to die and all human endeavour will ultimately fail, therefore I better get a shift on.'

Treat Death as your greatest ancestor.

Ignore Death – it'll go away.

Further Reading: *The Letters of John Keats*.

EXTREMES

(See **Prose**.)

Prose is not poetry.

Write your prose as if it were poetry.

Further Reading: James Joyce, *Finnegans Wake,* Faber.

FORMS

Forms is probably what Nick Royle was expecting me to write about, when he commissioned this piece.

'Extremely restrictive forms,' as Richard Beard – the only full Oulipian I've ever met – used to say, on the way to the University of East Anglia bar, after our Creative Writing classes with Malcolm Bradbury – 'are a way of generating text.'

You may or may not be the kind of writer for whom the idea of 'generating text' is appealing. I have moved away from sympathy with this, a little to my shame.

In the former Soviet Union, you and I would both have been called 'formalists' – because neither of us, I'm pretty sure, is a Socialist Realist. (And Richard Beard would already have been executed.)

Realise that all writing is restrictive. If you are writing a historical novel, you will have many things you can't do. But even if you choose to write in the first person, you will also have many necessary avoidances.

Express yourself – because you are beautiful, worthwhile, unimprovable.

Further Reading: Harry Mathews, Alastair Brotchie, Ian Monk, *The Oulipo Compendium*, Atlas Press.

GENRE

If you really want to make things difficult for yourself, try to write in an entirely new genre. Or conversely don't allow yourself to write in an existing genre. (Contemporary literary fiction is as much a genre as cat detective fiction. Take, for example, the subgenre of literary novels that mention fruit in their titles.)

Acknowledge that the genre is a bigger and stronger beast than you are. If you include a murder in your novel, it's a crime novel – and will be judged against other crime novels. However, just because something is a bigger and stronger beast than you doesn't mean that, by catching it off-balance, you can't flip it on its hairy arse.

Write as if you were bigger and more important than any genre, and didn't need to read genre fiction because it is beneath you.

Further Reading: Whatever is in the bestseller list this week.

HOTNESS

You will make things difficult for yourself by being unattractive. This is a shame as 'We are ugly but we have the music' was always one of the great compensations of art. In fact, it was the reason lots of us mingers fled towards aesthetic stuff in the first place. 'At least *this* stands a chance of making me interesting,' we thought. Preparation: days of emptiness during adolescence, no driving licence, no one to visit in the village. So, make something – a painting, a hat. And there in our postcard pantheons, George Eliot, Dostoievsky, Sartre – the blessedly pugly. But they didn't have to worry about whether or not their author photo was clickbait. Or whether, in the acquisition meeting at the publishers, their lack of marketability (euphemism) would be mentioned.

Write better than the pretty ones.

Surgery.

Further Listening: Janis Joplin.

INTERNET

I have a whole rant about this. Essentially, humans sitting at computers are less interesting as fictional subjects than humans doing almost anything else. It is possible that fiction as such will cease, and be replaced by game-playing, because so many of the possible human subjects are themselves playing games.

If it is your kind of thing, write about the contemporary world without ignoring but without being entirely dependent on communications technology. A face-to-face conversation is likely to play better with the reader than an exchange of texts or instant messages. The more isolated the protagonist, the harder they will be to write about entertainingly – the language describing them will become the Big Event, rather than any Big Event that happens to them.

Never go offline. Keep a chatbox open. Friend Tao Lin.

Further Reading: The internet.

'JOURNEY'

If you are prepared to refer to what you do, as a writer, in the vague-speak of Reality TV ('It's been a real journey and I've learned so much about myself') then you are making it difficult for yourself to be anything other than entirely shit.

Martin Amis made himself seem entirely *pretentious* by calling a book of his non-fiction writing *The War Against Cliché*. But Martin Amis was trying to be honest about the field in which writers, and thinkers, exist.

It is even more difficult to write without clichés of the soul than without clichés of expression.

Refuse to accept the common way of expressing anything.

Believe that human beings are more right about the world than they have ever been, and that human beings in the past were really stupid for not knowing all the stuff we know.

Further Reading: Apsley Cherry-Garrard, *The Worst Journey in the World*, Vintage.

KAFKA

You see, my Ancestors refuse to leave me alone. Kafka has no practical place here but he owns K. Go away, Franz.

Accept that you are not self-generating. Go for a walk in a graveyard.

Sit in Starbucks, writing, surrounded by notes, in the awareness that you will appear interesting to your fellow caffeinated artists.

Further Reading: Anne Carson, *If Not, Winter: Fragments of Sappho*, Virago.

LEGWORK/LIFE-THREATENING SITUATIONS

One of my blindspots is research, engagement, reportage. This would be, for me, a way of making difficult. Because I never willingly leave my writing room.

However, you may be a writer for whom writing is impossible without a basis of first-hand, physical knowledge. For something to become a subject for you, it may need to have damaged you.

Most writers, I would say, prefer engaging with fictional characters to engaging with real people (that's one of the reasons why they became writers). But the more you engage with real people, the better your characters will be. (I am saying this to myself as much as you.) The reason there are few good novels about manual labour is that writers are averse to it.

Put yourself where it is hard to remain.

Try to encounter people only like yourself.

Further Reading: Werner Herzog, *The Conquest of the Useless: Reflections from the Making of* Fitzcarraldo, Ecco.

MEDICATION

You may be on medication. You may need, for the rest of your life, to be on medication. You may also self-medicate. You may be an alcoholic or another kind of addict. This is one of the very best ways of making it difficult for yourself.

I am not going to say, 'Give it up,' – I am going to say, 'Think carefully about it.' In other words, be canny about the kind of writing you are likely to be able to achieve. Surf your manic states; hunker down through your glooms.

Realise that, without the particular kind of non-writing you do, the writing you do would not be the same.

Carry on just as you were.

Further Reading to Avoid at All Costs: David Foster Wallace, 'The Depressed Person', *Brief Interviews With Hideous Men*, Abacus.

NEWNESS

This is the obverse of **Ancestors**. They make it difficult by representing all they did that *you* have not done; making-it-newness makes it difficult by representing all you have not done that you need to do. (See **Obstacles**.)

Make it new.

Develop an elaborate argument that we are entering a new classical age – similar to the Seventeeth Century – in which furious originality is no longer a virtue. It is better, say, to provide your audience with exactly what they want rather than to pursue an estranging individualism.

Further reading: **Obstacles**.

OBSTACLES

A writer is only as original as her obstacles.

Examine closely what most contemporary writers think is not worth writing about. Write about it.

The only obstacles are the ones in the way of your career. As long as you can get a very large publishing deal, everything else will sort itself out.

Further Reading: Fernando Pessoa, *The Book of Disquiet*, Serpent's Tail.

PROSE

Prose is always a compromise. When you begin a 150,000-word novel, you make a deal with possibility. I have already mentioned **Death**, which may foreclose on your rich character development before your fragments are even interesting to your immediate family. But there is also a bargain with Time. I will voice it as well as I can: 'I can't spend the rest of my life perfecting every sentence in this one book. I am not Lampedusa. What I need is to get my prose-writing abilities up to a certain okay-ish level, and then I need to write at that level, saying roughly what needs to be said at each point, every day from now on until I have a first draft, after which I will (See **Rewriting**).' This includes a footnote: 'I am not trying to reinvent anything here. I want to write a writeable novel.' If you refuse to make this bargain, you are back to **Extremes** and **New**.

Write your prose as if it were a technical manual.

Write your prose as if it were poetry.

Further Reading: Flaubert, *Madame Bovary*, translated by Lydia Davis, Penguin, and Amy Hempel, *The Collected Stories*, Scribner.

QUIPS

When I am teaching Creative Writing (on the Birkbeck MA and elsewhere) I try, as much as possible, never to say never. Beginning writers get very bugged by nevers. 'Never open a novel with a description of miserable weather,' I once said. My students came back at me, the following Wednesday, with many examples of great novels that open with miserable weather. Some beginning writers read How To manuals in search of Nevers and Don'ts to add to their already long lists. Never use adverbs. Don't have your first-person narrator walk past a mirror, and notice and describe themselves, in the opening chapter of your book. Never make your hero an accountant. Don't use unexciting verbs! The truth is, if you are overly concerned about these things, you're not really focussing on what's important. Really great writers aren't prissy. As Orwell said, after laying out his verbotens, 'Break any of these rules sooner than say anything outright barbarous.' (Although the idea of creating something 'outright barbarous' always seemed to me a marvellous challenge. I think Orwell's barbarous was different to mine.)

Don't read How To manuals. Never collect superstitions.

Take Elmore Leonard extremely seriously.

Further reading: DH Lawrence's non-fiction.

REWRITING

Most of the things other people have said about rewriting are true. Almost certainly, none of them will come in all that handy when you're going back to the same paragraph for the fourteenth time. At that point what you need is stubbornness.

Read your writing as if you hadn't written it.

If you know what you're trying to say, and the words are there somewhere on the page, the reader will get it.

Further watching: *Le Mystère de Picasso* (*The Mystery of Picasso*) directed by Henri-Georges Clouzot.

SATIRE

If you really want to make it difficult for yourself, try to write politically. We need a proper satirist; not just a satirist of the language of power, but a satirist of the abuse of power. We know the powerful never misunderestimate the power of words. The abuse of power continues. We need to be appalled, not amused.

Believe that when you speak the whole world will listen and change for the better.

Believe that when you speak the whole world will listen and change for the better.

Further Reading: Karl Kraus, *Half Truths & One-and-a-Half Truths*, University of Chicago Press.

TECHNOLOGY

Technology that alters the human subject is important, otherwise it's trivial.

The novel in which every character could, at any moment,

contact every other character is very different from the novel in which they are phoneless and separated by uncrossable distances.

Ask yourself: is a novel decadent when dealing with subjects for whom issues of survival, hunger, harvest, are far off?

Don't be a magpie. Shiny things are not innately valuable.
When advertisers use the word 'Revolution', they mean it.

Further Reading: the early works of Douglas Coupland, particularly *Shampoo Planet*.

UNITED STATES

We all live in the United States unless we make the deliberate effort not to.

Write in an unAmerican way.

Only read American writers – they're the only game in town.

Further Reading: Chomsky.

VOICE

'Oh my God,' think most start-up writers, 'I need to find my voice. I need to find my voice as fast as I can. Until I find my unique, original, unmistakable voice, nothing I write will be worth anything.'

Let me be brutal: the greatest difficulty you will have is if you are a boring person. Or, if you have at any stage of your life accepted that you will endure a period of being boring in order to make enough money to become interesting later on.

In other words, you've become an accountant of the soul. This isn't to say that accountancy is evil. It is to say that, when most accountants begin speaking, most people stop listening. Artists are perpetually finding ways of making their art (the most important and enduring part of themselves) more fascinating. If you are not doing this, you are standing upright as the gun goes for the 100 metres final.

Most writers don't find a voice, I would argue. They find **Obstacles**. New ways of saying things demand new things that need to be said.

It's not how writers *say* the world, that's a relatively surface thing, it's how they *see* the world. If you see the world differently, you will need to find different ways of expressing what you see. However, if you are happy to admit that the world is already pretty much being seen as well as it can be, then you may as well give up. (In this previous sentence, you might choose to replace 'the world' with 'the genre of X'. Some writers' ambitions are limited, say, to the Extremely Violent Crime Novel rather than the world and all things in it.)

Find the blockages in language. What wants to be said?

Avoid reading entirely. You don't want to be influenced.

Further Reading: Virginia Woolf, *Selected Diaries* then all her diaries and letters.

WRITING

At the end of two years on the MA, one student said, 'You know, writing is hard.' All the tutors were delighted.

If you're in the shit, keep writing. As Randall Jarrell said, 'Each day brings its toad, each night its dragon.'

This will be the last piece of sarcastic advice: **Grow a pair, girls.**

X

The thing that is missing. The factor. You won't know what it is.

YADDO

That your writing circumstances are not perfect should be blamed for nothing. Even if you were on some juicy grant at Yaddo, they wouldn't be perfect either.

ZOMBIES

Zombies are unavoidable, so they had to come in here. They are as useful for my argument as zebras.

It is very easy to write as a zombie; it is very hard to write as a zebra.

EXERCISE

Write a dialogue in which A and B are discussing what C thinks of D. For the letters, insert the first first names you can think of. (Not existing fictional characters. Not real people.) Write the dialogue as if it were from a short story or novel, rather than from a script or screenplay. The more divergent the opinions, the more interesting the dialogue.

TOP TIPS

- Don't start collecting or getting hung up on all the 'Don'ts' and 'Nevers' you've picked up from other writers.
- Do be excessive in your first draft. You can't retrofit the excitement of discovery – and if the writer is discovering things at the moment of writing, the reader will feel them at the moment of reading. This has to happen first time through.
- As many times as you may have heard this: there are no short cuts. But, on the plus side: there is no wasted effort. If you find writing one story an almighty struggle, another – later – will flow so easily you'll think all writing is easy.

TEN 'DIFFICULT' – IN DIFFERENT WAYS – NOVELS

James Joyce, *Finnegans Wake*
Samuel Beckett, *Ill Seen, Ill Said*
David Foster Wallace, *The Pale King*
Muriel Spark, *Not to Disturb*
Virginia Woolf, *The Waves*
Eimear McBride, *A Girl is a Half-formed Thing*
Ben Marcus, *The Age of Wire and String*
Jack Kerouac, *On the Road: The Original Scroll*
David Markson, *this is not a novel*
Thomas Bernhard, *Wittgenstein's Nephew*

LIVI MICHAEL

APPROACHES TO THE
HISTORICAL NOVEL

R ECENTLY ONE OF my students showed me her writing
and asked 'Is it historical enough?' She was referring to
the fact that it was set in the 1980s.

It's not an uneducated question; historical fiction is notoriously difficult to define. The broadest definition was probably made by Jonathan Nield in 1902: 'Stories that in any
way whatsoever portray the life of the past even though actual
persons and actual public events play no part in them.'

In the rubric of the Walter Scott Prize, however, a historical
novel is one in which 'the majority of the events described take
place at least 60 years before the publication of the novel, and
therefore stand outside any mature personal experience of the
author,' ('60 years' refers to Scott's novel *Waverley, Or 'Tis
Sixty Years Since'*).

Historical fiction is also distinguished from memoir in
the definition applied by the Historical Novel Society: 'To
be deemed historical (in our sense), a novel must have been
written at least fifty years after the events described, or have
been written by someone who was not alive at the time of

those events (who therefore approaches them only by research).'

Since my student was writing about events that occurred before her lifetime I decided that her story fulfilled the criteria.

The time frame is not the only problem, however, when it comes to establishing the boundaries of the genre. Sarah Johnson's *Historical Fiction: A Guide to the Genre* (2005) has 3800 entries, which include only novels written between 1995 and 2004, and set before the twentieth century.

The burgeoning category of historical fiction contains romances such as those written by Georgette Heyer, Jean Plaidy and various Mills & Boon authors; adventure stories written by Patrick O'Brian and Bernard Cornwell; and crime fiction written by Ellis Peters or CJ Sansom. The trend towards historical crime may reflect the fact that the process of uncovering history is in itself a kind of investigation. An early example is *The Daughter of Time* by Josephine Tey. When Scotland Yard inspector Alan Grant is confined to bed with a broken leg, he begins to investigate the alleged murder of the princes in the Tower by Richard III. This novel explores how history is constructed and how certain versions of history prevail (in this case, Tudor over Plantagenet).

In *The Name of the Rose,* by Umberto Eco, William de Baskerville investigates a series of murders in a medieval monastery. A historical murder mystery combining semiotics with philosophy and literary theory, Eco's novel cannot be said to belong purely to any one genre. However, it presents historical investigation as a flawed search for truth and meaning. Another literary writer, John Banville, writing as Benjamin Black, uses his historical mysteries in a more political way, to uncover the abuses of the Catholic Church.

It is possible to find all the major literary trends of the

twentieth century in historical fiction. In Virginia Woolf's modernist classic, *Orlando*, for instance, the central character lives from Tudor times to the present day. Orlando doesn't die, but does change gender. Woolf creates an image of the 'self' that is multiple and unconfined: 'a biography is considered complete if it merely accounts for six or seven selves; a person may have as many as a thousand.'

Jeanette Winterson infuses magic realism into history in *The Passion* (1987). Set during the Napoleonic Wars, this novel intertwines the stories of Henri, a French soldier, and Villanelle, the red-haired, web-footed daughter of a Venetian boatman, whose husband has (literally) gambled away her heart. By contrast, Susannah Clarke's *Jonathan Strange and Mr Norrell* (2004) sets the Napoleonic Wars in the context of a suppressed history of magic in a pastiche of both historical narrative and the eighteenth-century novel.

The historical novel is perhaps most frequently used as a vehicle for the suppressed voice. Writers such as Toni Morrison, Sarah Waters, Andrea Levy and Colm Tóibín focus on the stories and people that have been written out of history. The voices of their characters, black, gay, dispossessed, contest Churchill's famous claim that 'history is written by the victors'. The post-colonial historical novel could form a genre of its own. In *Things Fall Apart* (1959), for instance, Chinua Achebe graphically portrays the problems and conflicts within Nigeria after independence from empire.

Wide Sargasso Sea (1966) is one of my favourite post-colonial classics but is also part of another sub-genre, in which fiction is derived explicitly from fiction. In this novel Jean Rhys re-tells the story of *Jane Eyre*, giving a voice to Rochester's first wife in a powerful critique of colonial imperialism. Similarly, in *Song of Achilles* (2012), Madeline Miller takes a canonical text, *The Iliad*, and re-tells it using the voice of Patroclus in a passionate evocation of the love between Patroclus and Achilles.

The historical novel, therefore, may offer alternative histories, and within the genre there is also alternative fiction such as Thomas Harris' *Fatherland* (1992) which explores a scenario in which the Nazis were successful in the Second World War. Kate Atkinson's *Life After Life* (2013) offers a distinctive variation on this theme, portraying multiple versions of a single life.

Novels such as *Hawksmoor* by Peter Ackroyd or *The Time Traveller's Wife* by Audrey Niffenegger move between a contemporary and a historical setting, while George RR Martin famously draws on the Wars of the Roses to create his fantasy world in *Game of Thrones*. Do we include these novels in the same general category?

Post-modern writers such as Eco, Ackroyd or Ian McEwan use pastiche, metafiction, fragmentation and ellipsis to draw attention to history as narrative. Compelling but not authoritative, history exists as one account among others and is always open to question. Contemporary historical fiction, therefore, has come a long way from the historical romance. It tends to be formally experimental, non-linear, emphasising the marginalised voice, or voices, and the rewriting of established history. *The Night Watch*, by Sarah Waters, uses a reverse chronology, from 1947 to 1941, for instance, while in *Life After Life* Ursula Todd's history is told time and again, from her birth in 1910, to any one of several deaths.

Given that the field is so varied, if you want to write historical fiction, where do you begin?

By reading, of course. Read as much as you can and gradually you will develop a sense of what you enjoy and what can be done with the historical novel. It is an interesting exercise, for instance, to contrast two novels by Hilary Mantel and CJ Sansom: *Bring Up the Bodies* (2012) and *Lamentation* (2014). These writers are writing about the same period and similar characters while taking a radically different approach. If you read the first page of each you will see the difference immediately. Mantel's opening is much more tangential, tending to wrong-foot the reader, whereas *Lamentation* takes you straight into the plot. When we read the first line of *Bring Up the Bodies* – 'His daughters are falling from the sky' – we know we have to engage in an act of interpretation. Thomas Cromwell's daughters are not literally *falling from the sky*, but we are taken immediately into his perspective, and remain in it throughout the novel, charmed into empathetic identification with a henchman or mass murderer. In the extraordinary opening paragraph, dramatic movement, shifting territory and scale and the imagery of blood tells us metaphorically about the rest of the novel.

The first line of *Lamentation* is also a short, declarative sentence: 'I did not want to attend the burning.' Matthew Shardlake is immediately established as a humane individual somewhat at odds with his social milieu. As an investigative lawyer, he is well placed to introduce us to a multi-faceted and layered Tudor society. The plot unfolds in the logical, sequential way of detective fiction, revealing more of the world in which it is set at each stage. Despite similarities, Mantel and Sansom are aiming at an entirely different readership; the book you prefer may indicate the kind of readership you want.

A third kind of approach is taken by Sarah Waters, who, in her first three novels, consciously draws on works by Dickens, Wilkie Collins and others to create a version of the nineteenth century which is several shades darker than any Victorian novel. In *Fingersmith* (2002), for instance, we find subject matter that is implicit, or between the lines of Victorian fiction:

sexual love between women, baby-farming, pornography and the brutality of asylums. The first line of the novel – 'My name, in those days, was Susan Trinder' – draws attention to a Dickensian underworld of deceit and to the theme of shifting, duplicitous identity.

Bring Up the Bodies is based around historical figures; the characters in *Fingersmith* are entirely fictional. In *Lamentation*, Sansom moves between the two. The choice you make, whether to dramatise actual historical events and characters or to give a historical setting to an imaginary story and characters, will depend on whether you want to revise history by reinterpretation or by supplementation.

When you portray a character that already exists, you are arguably more constrained than if you are inventing one. However, if you want to make this character compelling and convincing, you will need to portray him/her in moments that are outside history or between the lines: moments of intimacy, reflection, turning points, secret fears and desires. If you begin with a known character such as Richard III, you will need to ask questions that are not about his known history, for example who do you trust? Were you ever afraid of the dark? What do you dream about? This should enable you to find a unique way into his story and bring him to life for your reader.

It's one of the great challenges of historical fiction to make the reader believe the unbelievable or extraordinary. Cecily Neville, Duchess of York, for instance, gave birth to thirteen children, only two of whom outlived her. Two of her sons became king; one of them executed his brother and the other (allegedly) murdered his brother's children after usurping the throne.

You couldn't make it up. Or if you did, you might be told to tone it down. The historical novelist has to rewrite these sensational histories in such a way that makes them fresh, compelling and convincing for each new generation of readers.

Truth is stranger than fiction. And the truth of historical fiction is supported by research. Many historical novelists are drawn to the field by a love of research. However, research may actually constitute an obstacle to producing a really good novel. Not one in which the dialogue is overloaded with information, that contains page after page of descriptive setting or in which extra facts are somewhat awkwardly winched in, but one in which we are drawn in to a different world without being aware of the research.

Research creates a sense of authenticity, and may also provide a kind of scaffold or structure for the novel. The reader has to believe in the world you create, but there is an interesting negotiation in historical fiction between familiarisation and de-familiarisation. The world of the novel has to be convincingly alien while containing elements that the reader can relate to. Often the familiarising elements are personal and psychological – ambition, betrayal, love – whereas de-familiarisation tends to occur through the settings and events.

It is necessary, therefore, to do enough research to be able to use it as a springboard for your story; to give the impression, at least, that your characters live and breathe in the medium of their world. It is not necessary to spend days looking up the kind of furniture polish used in eighteenth-century Latvia, or who branded the royal swans. Don't get hung up on detail. In almost every case your novel will work as well or better without it. Most novels are improved by cutting things out. And you need to trust the imagination of your reader. So be meticulous in your research; adopt a method that works for you and stick to it systematically. Then leave it behind.

EXERCISE

Some historical novels are based around paintings, for example Tracy Chevalier's *Girl With a Pearl Earring*. The work of art may be used in different ways – as a trigger for plot as in Josephine Tey's *The Daughter of Time*, or symbolically, as in Sarah Dunant's *Birth of Venus*, in which the painting represents the 'birth' or development of a female artist in sixteenth-century Florence. You might like to select a painting from the era that you are writing about, but for the purpose of this exercise I'm going to use *The Venus of Urbino* (1538) by Titian.

- Look at the painting.
- What does it suggest to you about the period?
- What can you deduce from the setting?
- Focus on the background to the right of the central figure. What do you see?
- Write twelve sentences describing what you see, drawing in your focus more closely with each one.
- Select one of the two figures.
- Think of six questions that you could ask this person.
- Now select one of the sentences you have written as a possible opening, and base a story around the answer to at least one of your questions.

TOP TIPS

- Do not rely on the historical events themselves for structuring your novel. Have a strong story arc planned in advance – preferably before researching your novel.
- Do your research then ruthlessly cut it out.
- Use modern dialogue with elisions, for example 'you've', 'didn't' etc. Anything else just sounds falsely archaic.

TEN FAVOURITE HISTORICAL NOVELS

The Playmaker (1987) Thomas Kenneally
Beloved (1990) Toni Morrison
Restoration (1989) Rose Tremain
Regeneration (1991) Pat Barker
Atonement (2001) Ian McEwan
The Master (2004) Cólm Toibín
Christine Falls (2007) Benjamin Black
The Night Watch (2006) Sarah Waters
The Stranger's Child (2011) Alan Hollinghurst
Bring Up the Bodies (2012) Hilary Mantel

JOE STRETCH

COMING OF AGE

THAT'S ME, NATHAN Bates – I'm the one dancing by the burning microwave, brandishing a femidom, wearing a pink mankini, the gusset of which, if memory serves, is speckled with cocaine. That red Doc Martens boot in the bottom left corner, that belongs to Lola. Her foot's inside it. Her lovely left foot. What you can't see is the copy of *Crime and Punishment* she's holding. Oh, Lola Kelsey. Lovely Lola Kelsey. The girl who read at house parties. The girl who ruined my life.

Novels or stories that begin like this unnerve me. They remind me of running on the spot. Beware, when writing, of running on the spot. You'll know you're doing it if:

Your story doesn't go anywhere, despite a lot of effort.

When you read over your story you can almost feel your text getting tired, as the paragraphs pass by, you can sense their energy draining, from that hyperactive opening one to the one, some pages later, that's so fatigued you feel sick and sleepy on its behalf.

For years my attempts at writing novels were all abandoned after roughly six thousand words. I couldn't understand why.

I felt 'the voice' was okay. 'Things' seemed to be 'happening'. But it didn't go anywhere.

I came up with rules. Maybe they will be useful, or maybe you can come up with your own rules. Mine were these:

Beware of false energy.

I get a bit worried if something 'seems exciting', because it creates the expectation that something will 'be exciting'. Beware of what you promise. No one will forgive you when you fail to deliver. (Oh my god, you'll never guess what happened . . .) Why not create the expectation that nothing's going to happen? Then it'll be a lovely surprise when something does. Literature is fuelled by the ordinary. The ordinary is the name we give to the world we don't understand.

The page is not a stage.

Beware of writing, particularly in the first person, as if you're standing in a spotlight, performing yourself. The page is intimate. Picture a mouth whispering to an ear. Hear the cautious timbre of someone telling the truth. What we're trying to avoid is that sinking feeling we experience when someone says to us, 'My name's Pete. I'm the kind of person who just says what I think to your face.' Or, 'I'm Carol. The thing about me is . . .'

There are always exceptions.

In fact, you might see all rules in writing as similar to those wet planks of wood you find in abandoned industrial spaces. It's your job to lift the plank (the rule) up, and to observe the startled worms and insects underneath.

That analogy might feel incomplete.

But I promise it isn't.

When I was twenty-two I figured something out. Don't try and express yourself. Don't try and find yourself. Don't try to reveal yourself. I sought instead to destroy myself. Writing as a kind of low-key, recreational suicide.

This helped in a few ways.

My dreams and ambitions became my material rather than my motivation. Overnight the subtext of my work went from being 'This is a story written by a young person who loves literature but doesn't understand it and would love to be a considered *a good writer*', to being, well, something else. Which was progress.

Around the same time I was also able to admit to myself how desperate I was to have sex. Once I confessed to myself that my identity was a blown and badly painted egg, lots of other things started to appear in the subtext of my writing. Again, things I understood less and had less control over.

So the lesson here is this: don't try to perfect yourself in your writing, or articulate a perfected version of yourself, who you'd be if the world hadn't intervened. Don't try to be someone; be aware you're no one.

I'm writing about this because your attitude, or your approach to writing, will flood your subtext from word one, so you need to know if you're toxic or not. Your very desire to write might well make you toxic. *Why* do you want to write? I've seen many a wonderful raconteur get buried in a paper coffin. No matter what you write on it, a page will find ways of displaying your ambition. So be clear what your ambitions are. To tell a story is a good ambition. To be big-hearted with your characters is a good ambition. To treat the reader with respect. To be honest. To be generous with your imagery. To be attentive to the world where your characters live. To be aware that you don't know everything. To be aware that you don't know what you yourself are like. To be aware that if people witnessed your private self they'd probably recognise themselves, more so than your public self. This is the stuff to be thinking about. Or at least it might help to improve things.

Your story is the horse you're sitting on. If it's standing still, maybe give it a gentle kick. If it's already walking, maybe just see where it goes.

I'd rather think of the page as a vertical thing than a horizontal one. What I mean is, I prefer to think in terms of depth, rather than length. Wordcount, therefore, is a largely meaningless number. People love wordcount; they're crazy. If you find yourself tweeting how many words you've written in a given day, worry. Don't freak out. Just worry.

I don't know how you measure the depth of a text exactly. I do it by reading my sentence aloud and seeing how I feel. If I feel depressed and like a hideous fraud, that's a bad sign. If I feel like someone's pressing a two pound coin against my metasternum, then I feel pretty hopeful. If I find myself delighting in every syllable of the sentence then I get breathless and feel worried but I leave the sentence alone and plan to judge it some other time.

The only way I know to generate depth is to delete approximately 97 per cent of the words I write. Sometime I spend months trying to write 97 per cent fewer words. And this never works. Rather, it results in paragraphs that remind me of a rattlesnake's skin my Auntie Rita found in Las Vegas. (Brittle.)

The letters keys on the keyboard are fine. They're great. But whether you're a decent writer or not will be dictated by your relationship with the delete key. The more sophisticated and intimate your relationship with this key, the better you'll write. So attend to this button as you did the girl or boy whom you fixated on when you were young. That person you would have done almost anything for. To see them, wandering

JOE STRETCH

round school, or in the street. How that felt. How physical
and painful and great. The delete key is your lover now. If you
don't want to have sex with it then still try to see it as the most
beautiful tool – like those lovely brushes archaeologists use to
excavate urns.

The coming-of-age novel is a genre. So you should be aware of
generic expectations. Otherwise you might find yourself simply conforming to them, rather than 'handling' them. Really,
to write a genre is to subvert it. The only real choice is how
gentle or radical you are.

There'll be a school. There'll be an obsession with a girl
or a boy. There'll be a mildly histrionic mother. There'll be a
distant father. One of them might well be an alcoholic. There'll
be a best friend. There'll be a coolish older sibling. There'll be
a bully of some kind. There'll be a pet. These are the things
it's tough to avoid. The main thing is to do *more* than this. To
avoid these things. If this is all you've got, worry. But don't
freak out.

In terms of narrative: your main character is going to betray
their parents, be betrayed by their parents and do a series
of embarrassing or maybe disturbing things involving shit,
piss, semen, mud and alcohol. They're going to have sex, or
not.

In novels, things and people come together and there's drama. In a coming-of-age novel a young person alights from
the ghost train of family life and runs towards that bright
strip of light, the world. They're full of hopes, most of which
will be dashed. This is your story. How are you going to tell
it?

Other traps to fall into include:

You're writing a story in the first person and your narrator is 'hyper self-aware' or, 'really observant' or 'really clever and neurotic'. I'm not saying don't do these things. But your awareness that these are well-trodden paths might encourage you to walk them in your own way.

The love interest. The girl will read interesting books or like music you've never heard of but seems cool. She will be an outsider, perhaps even the victim of unsevere bullying by more conventional young people. She will be taciturn and beautifully unbeautiful. The boy will be even more taciturn, yet might occasionally conform to young male stereotypes in ways that make you wonder what he's really like, and why you love him. Be careful. Remember your reader fixated on people and longed for love as desperately as you did.

My family owned a microwave. I've never seen a femidom. I used to like the idea of a girl who read at house parties, which is a ridiculous thing really.

Childhood often comes to life on the page. Something about how we experienced it – our hunger for it. Start writing about childhood and invariably it begins to feel like material. The dangers emerge when we try to *honour*, or do justice to, specific events and people. Don't get so bogged down in the actual that you forget to tell a story. There will be lies. And they'll feel like deeper truths.

Carry a dictionary. Look up words you already know.

Say to yourself, Read, you twat. It's what you love.

The problem of masturbation can be a problem.

Make no mistake, when people say 'writing is editing', they're right.

The better you get, the worse you feel.

Ask yourself, If I deleted this chapter and rewrote it from scratch, would it be better? Ask yourself that and be utterly honest with your reply. Ask yourself out loud on your own.

Crave the heroin of criticism.

I do believe, increasingly, that writing should be fun, even when you feel hurt and angry and sad.

A day of writing starts with hope. At lunchtime it feels like you're onto something. In the evening you're the most embarrassing person that ever lived.

Get up early.

Go to bed late.

EXERCISE

Write sincerely about yourself from the perspective of one of your parents.

TOP TIPS

- Don't just mindlessly read your work aloud to yourself. Set your soul to 'Maximum Sensitivity', then read it aloud. And when you get that sinking feeling, respond to it, think, make adjustments.
- Postpone breakfast.
- Experiment. For example, put four full stops in a sentence and examine their different effects.

TEN GREAT COMING-OF-AGE BOOKS

The Bell Jar – Sylvia Plath
My Fault – Billy Childish
Le Grand Meaulnes – Alain-Fournier
Nightspawn – John Banville
Great Expectations – Charles Dickens
The Cement Garden – Ian McEwan
A Girl is a Half-Formed Thing – Eimear McBride

Franny & Zooey – JD Salinger
Never Let Me Go – Kazuo Ishiguro
I Capture the Castle – Dodie Smith

JAMES MILLER

THE IMPORTANCE OF PLACE
AND SETTING IN THE NOVEL

A NOVEL MUST be set somewhere. It must have a location in both time and space. The location of the novel
determines what we might call its field of possibility: it helps
to establish the sort of characters you can write about and
the things that might happen to them. As a result, place and
setting are inseparable from plot and for this reason, if you
don't handle place and setting properly, your novel will fail. It
doesn't matter if your novel is set in the present, past or future,
in a real place, a wholly fictional one or a fictional place based
on real places. Nor does it matter whether your novel concerns itself with a specific, localised territory or ranges far and
wide, but as the author you need to know not only *why* your
novel is set in one place or another, you must also know this
place, know it as intimately as you know your own home. Fur-
thermore, the intimate, domestic and internal spaces of your
character's world are just as significant as the wider, external
world they move through. As the French philosopher Gaston
Bachelard wrote, 'our house is our corner of the world', and
so it makes a tremendous difference to your character if he

or she was born in a cottage or a mansion, if they live in one particular street rather than another. Remember: environment always helps to determine character.

Therefore, when planning the location of your novel, you need to break this location into its component parts. There is the wider setting – what we might call the backdrop – which will be the nation, the city, the landscape. But there are also local issues of place and setting: the neighbourhood where your character is based, the house where they live and, within that, the layout and decoration of the rooms. The wider, external environment helps shape your characters and the options available to them: it *forms* them. The smaller, more intimate environment of your character's private space is an *expression* of their personality and circumstance: are they neat or messy, ostentatious or refined, rich or poor? You might even write a novel about a character that spends their entire time in airports, airplanes and hotels – the non-spaces of the globalised world – and you might never show their home town or their apartment. It doesn't matter – you, as the author, still need to know these things about your character, even if they never feature in the actual novel. What we choose to omit is just as important as what we include.

Place and setting represent more than just the external arena of your novel. They are not just a neutral, picturesque backdrop. Just as there is nowhere in the actual world free from history or separate from social and economic forces, so your fictional location is also bound up with these ideological issues. Location is political. Location is also symbolic and metaphoric: it stands for something greater than itself. If handled properly, the use of place in your novel will resonate and reflect the wider themes that your plot should explore. Nor should strategic use of a particular location bind or limit your novel to a parochial concern. Rather the location should resonate with a much greater and arguably more universal quality. This chapter will consider a few practical ways to explore these issues and suggest how we can best immerse ourselves in our fictional locations.

First, you need to know why your story is set in one particular place rather than another. If you don't know why, that would suggest you need to think much harder about the book you want to write. Every city, town or village, every field or mountain has its own particular genius, its specific character. But this immediately raises an issue: as a writer, is it your responsibility to try and capture the particular 'truth' of a place? Not necessarily. This might be the case for travel writers or journalists but as a novelist the problem is rather more a case of how to *use* a location to the best advantage of a story. It is not so much that you are trying to represent a place in the most accurate way. Rather, you are *interpreting* a place, representing it in a way that best suits the mood and the deeper meaning of your novel. For example: Thomas Hardy created Wessex, a fictionalised area of the UK based on the West Country to show how the conflicts and crises that assailed his protagonists were bound up with changes taking place in late nineteenth-century England, changes that were inseparable from changes to the environment that surrounded his characters, a landscape that was caught between the modern and the traditional, the rural and the emerging urban-industrial. Hardy was able to express a particular West Country vernacular, to dwell very much in the particularity of his specific location and, at the same time, show how this location also stood for much larger concerns. Rather than limiting his work, Hardy's immersion in the particular was a way of expanding the significance of his novels. We could say the same about Dickens' London, Hugo's Paris, Dostoyevsky's St Petersburg, Faulkner's Yoknapatawpha county, Tolkein's Middle Earth and so on.

Some creative writing tutors argue that you should not try to write about places you do not know or have not visited. They would say that if you live in a small town in Cornwall you should write only about Cornwall and not – for example – the slums of Mumbai. Whilst there is a degree of truth to this opinion, it's not one I entirely endorse. There should be no limit, geographic or otherwise, to our imaginative reach. But at the same time, it's important that our readers remain convinced. A novelist should never be very worried about 'telling the truth'. There are no truths, after all, only versions of the truth. Novelists are all liars and thieves: the important thing is that the lies we tell are convincing and the details we steal to build our fictional worlds are the right ones. If your work lacks vision then your location will fail to convince or interest your reader, even if you write about the place where you have spent your entire life. Knowing a place and being able to write about it are by no means the same.

So, how best to write about a familiar location? The immediate advantage is that it should be a place you know very well – the place you can see out of your window as you sit at your desk. But that doesn't necessarily make it easier to write about. Sometimes, when a place is too familiar we forget how to 'see' it. We need to find a way to make it seem fresh and new, we need to find a way to see it as if for the first time. Or, rather, to perceive it like our characters do. As a result, many of the techniques that can be used to write about an unfamiliar place apply equally to the familiar. These techniques can be summarised as follows: walks; photographs; maps; reading and research. Let's consider each technique in turn.

As a writer, it's important to walk. Walking, along with reading (and, of course, writing), is one of the best things you can do, whether it be a simple meditative stroll around your favourite park or a psychogeographical romp through stranger territories. As Robert Macfarlane notes, in many cultures 'walking and knowing are barely divisible activities' and the relationship between thinking and walking is deeply grained into the history of the English language itself: the etymological root/route of the word 'to learn' is 'to follow a track'. If you can, you need to walk around the place where your novel is set as much as possible. Look at the people and the architecture. Take your time. Sit in cafes, observe and listen. Absorb. Try to notice things. What seems to be going on and what is actually going on. Think about your characters. How would they walk around these streets? What shops would they go to? Which house would they live in? Scout out locations as if you were going to make a movie. This is where photographs come in. With smart phones it has never been easier to take pictures. Photograph everything. Find the sort of house you think your character would live in or the place where they might work, and photograph it. Many of these locations will exist first in your imagination. The challenge is to find them in real life. For example, in the novel I'm currently writing there is a scene where two of the characters squat an empty mansion in Mayfair. I knew exactly what the mansion looked like and after writing a version of the scene I walked around Mayfair, camera-phone in hand, until I found exactly the place that my characters were going to infiltrate. Keeping a photographic record is useful as well if your novel is set in a place you don't often visit, acting as an excellent supplement to memory.

Go for walks at unusual times. Get up before dawn and go for a walk while the streets are still empty and the light is different. Listen to music as you walk to change your mood. Cautiously imbibe stimulants or psychedelics. Use technological applications – filters and effects – to distort the photographs you take of a particular place in order to capture not just the fact of a place but the way a place *feels*. Remember, you are not striving for documentary objectivity but an interpretation suitable to the mood and theme of your novel.

Maps are useful enablers. Maps allow you to visualise your location in a different way. Read maps as avidly as you might read a book. Stare at them. Internalise the landscape. Combine, in your imagination, the actual space you've explored on foot with the cartographic representation of the space. In this way you can begin to build up a detailed mental map of the space of your novel, allowing the actual space to merge with your imaginative, internal vision. With Google Earth and Google Street View it has never been easier to explore the world and these are essential tools, particularly to help you realise distant and unfamiliar settings. What does that particular LA street corner look like? Now you can find out.

Old-fashioned reading and research are also important. When writing about a particular place, you need to know how other authors have represented it. If your novel is set in Venice, for example, then your representation of the city will be filtered through every other representation of that city. You can't escape these influences, so don't even try. The best you can do is to be aware. It's always a good idea to do a little research into the history of the place you are writing about as this research often uncovers hidden nuggets of information that you can use in your novel, further deepening and expanding your understanding of your location.

With fantastic or entirely imaginary locations, the same rules apply. You might be writing a fantasy novel set in a surreal, mountainous landscape, or a science fiction novel set on a distant planet. Invariably, even the most fantastic and impossible places derive from actual locations in the real world: we can never invent anything entirely new. Rather we create new things by combining actually existing things and places.

Your fantasy landscape might actually resemble Tibet, while your futuristic mega-city will relate to every other futuristic mega-city you've ever read about in other novels or comics or seen at the cinema.

I faced numerous challenges to do with location and setting in my second novel, *Sunshine State*, which was set almost entirely in a post-apocalyptic Florida. But I wrote it while living in London and Buenos Aires. I knew exactly why the novel had to be set in Florida even though using such an unfamiliar setting raised numerous problems. If I got the setting wrong, I knew I would get the whole novel wrong. First, I bought detailed maps of the state and spent a lot of time on Google Earth, tracing the journey my character was supposed to make, trying to identify the places where he would stop and assessing the distances between scenes. How long would it take to cross on foot, by boat or buggy? I was not entirely concerned with verisimilitude: after all, in my dystopic vision extreme climate change had substantially altered the environment and my hero was an outsider so his confusion and uncertainty acted as a suitable foil to cover some of my own doubts about this location. But I still had to get the setting right, I had to make sure my readers would be convinced.

After I'd done all the research and had written most of my first draft I flew to Atlanta and recreated my protagonist's journey to Miami. This on-the-ground experience was invaluable. It gave me a much stronger sense of space and distance. I was able to get crucial details about actual buildings – a hotel in Disneyworld, for example, that featured in one chapter – exactly right. Seeing the buildings showed me how much my imagination got wrong and made me realise that certain scenes would have to be handled quite differently. The climax of the novel was set in Miami, albeit a Miami destroyed by constant storms and now mainly inhabited by criminal gangs, religious maniacs and dangerous insurgents. The actual experience of driving across the bay from downtown to Miami Beach, for example, made me grasp the true scale of the city and realise how tough this would be for my hero to accomplish on foot and in dangerous circumstances. The finale was set in a ruined skyscraper. I identified the skyscraper (a recently completed condominium building) and even tried (but eventually failed) to access the building and visit the penthouse where the final showdown took place. Ideally, I would have rented a flat and stayed in Miami for a couple of months and it's possible that such immersion would have improved my novel, but either way, the trip – coupled with the huge stash of photographs I took for later reference – allowed me to best realise the setting of the novel and finish the book properly.

EXERCISE

The following exercise uses music to unlock our creativity. For the exercise, you need to select a piece of abstract, ambient music, preferably a piece that lacks obvious signifiers: it should have no vocals, avoid obvious minor or major key progressions, avoid certain types of beat (or have no beat at all), avoid obvious climaxes or movements. I like to use a fifteen-minute piece called 'In the Fog' by Tim Hecker, but there are lots of similar compositions. The piece is in many ways analogous to abstract art: it induces a mood, but this mood is very much open to interpretation. Some students find the piece beautiful, others depressing. For some it is crowded and overwhelming, for others it seems minimal and restrained. Once the music starts, students should not try to consciously 'think' about the music: they should avoid conscious thought as much as possible and just start writing whatever comes to mind, following a chain of associations and moods. I've always found this a very productive exercise – within minutes the entire room falls into a trance and a lot of very interesting writing then emerges.

TOP TIPS

- Read as widely and deeply as you can. Read everything, especially the classics and the more marginalised, less obvious texts. Avoid mass-market best-sellers or 'books of the moment' that everyone is reading as the popularity of these texts usually means they contain dead ideas and dead language. Difficult books are often more rewarding – embrace the difficulty, it will enlarge your mind to new possibilities.
- Try to keep a steady routine. Abandon the romantic fallacy that writers have disordered lives full of drama and chaos. Your characters will have disordered, chaotic lives. You're not a character in a novel, you're writing the novel. Serious work requires calm and focus.
- Learn to meditate. It will help you achieve calm and focus and it can help synchronise the left and right sides of your brain, fusing your creativity with your ability to structure and plan.

TEN NOVELS THAT CHANGED THE
WAY I THINK ABOUT NOVELS

Roberto Bolaño, *2666*
Cormac McCarthy, *Blood Meridian*
Philip Roth, *My Life As a Man*
Jeet Thayil, *Narcopolis*
Richard Ford, *Canada*
Edith Wharton, *The Custom of the Country*

THE IMPORTANT OF PLACE AND SETTING

James Baldwin, *Another Country*
Tom Bullough, *Konstantin*
Lorrie Moore, *A Gate at the Stairs*
JM Coetzee, *Waiting For the Barbarians*

SARAH BUTLER

PLAYING THE LONG GAME

I WROTE A lot as a kid; then I stopped; then I started again, aged 23, because I realised if I didn't take this thing seriously then I would regret it. The story's longer and more convoluted than that, but you get the general gist.

My first novel, *Ten Things I've Learnt About Love* (which is actually my third – we'll come to that), was bought when I was 34. I make that 11 years. Eleven years of writing, reading, studying for an MA in creative writing, writing, finishing a novel, getting an agent, not getting a book deal, writing, reading, finishing another novel, losing an agent, failing to get another agent, writing, reading, finishing another novel, and eventually – a combination of hard work and serendipity – getting a book deal.

Eleven years is a long time. There were moments during that time when I felt desperate: I wanted to be published, more than anything in the world, and yet it seemed endlessly, frustratingly, impossibly out of reach. I write this with two novels published by Picador, and a lovely bunch of foreign rights deals thrown in. I worked hard, and I was lucky – but most of all, I am where I am because I didn't give up. I found ways to sustain myself: ways of thinking; ways of writing; even ways of earning money for writing. The first novel Picador published was the third I had written. Writing one novel is a long, hard, lonely process, especially when you have no idea if it will ever see the light of day. Writing three is, well, writing three. I don't have a formula, or a template, but I have learnt some things along the way.

VALIDATION HELPS

After it became evident that my first novel was not going to sell I realised that I needed to get something published – I wanted to be read; I wanted to see my words in print; I wanted reassurance that I wasn't on some crazy wild goose chase; I wanted validation. So I turned my attention to short stories: sending one after the other off until I had one accepted by Route for inclusion in their *Wonderwall* anthology. They even paid me – not very much, but it was the best money I had ever earned. It boosted my confidence, and I returned to novel writing with a spring in my step.

FOCUSING ON THE PROCESS INSTEAD OF THE GOAL WILL PROBABLY HELP YOU GET NEARER THE GOAL

With the first two novels I wrote, my focus, if I'm honest, was on getting published. I was in a rush, hungry for a book with my name on the front. I have always admired my good friend Emma Claire Sweeney, also a novelist, for the amount of time and attention she gives to her writing, her determination to make her work the very best it can be, however long that takes. Inspired by her, when I started *Ten Things I've Learnt About Love* I made a conscious promise to myself that I would let this novel take as long as it needed to take and that my ambition was to write the best book I could, regardless. I relaxed, I stopped rushing, I spent time working out what I was trying to do and rewrote and restructured for years (five to be precise). It is a better book than the other two. I enjoyed writing it. It is also published.

YOU ARE ALWAYS LEARNING, ALWAYS IMPROVING

Writers are lucky: we can write for five, ten, twenty, fifty years without breaking into the market, and – frustrating as that might be – all that time we are practising our craft, we are getting better, we are upping our chances of getting noticed. We are working out how we write (everyone does it differently as far as I can gather), we are experimenting, learning, finding new stories and new ways of telling them. Spare a thought for actors and athletes who don't have time on their side in the way we do. We can write without permission, without theatres or auditions, without expensive equipment or tuition. We can go to our local library and borrow books which will teach us what we need to know if we pay attention and read closely. Those eleven years and the who knows how many hundreds of thousands of words I wrote during them all helped; not one was a waste of time.

GENEROSITY BREEDS GENEROSITY

In 2011, I had written *Ten Things I've Learnt About Love*. I couldn't get an agent. I was feeling fairly miserable about the whole thing. I worked for a summer in Cambridge, teaching creative writing to American students – part of my portfolio of workshops, residencies, projects. While I was there, Francesca Main, an editor at Simon and Schuster, who was just about to move to Picador, came to do an event for our students. We chatted. I spoke about my project work and my own writing and my current (futile) attempts to find an agent. Francesca asked to read my novel. Which never happens, right? Except it did. A year or so later – after I had seriously rewritten my novel in response to her feedback and she had offered me a two-book deal (without an agent in sight), after Picador had sold my novel in fifteen countries – I asked why she had asked to read my manuscript. She said that she liked my attitude, that she could tell from the way I spoke that I took my writing seriously, she was interested in what little I had told her about my novel, and she was inspired by the way I had built a life and career rooted in my enthusiasm for writing and stories.

An alternative heading for this ramble might be 'make sure you network' or 'it helps to know the right people' but there's a reason I've chosen to mention generosity. I find in all areas of my life that the more you share, the more others share; the more open and honest you are, the more life offers you. I did not connect with Francesca because she was an editor and I wanted a publishing deal; I connected with her because I was passionate about writing and literature.

THERE ARE OTHER WAYS OF BEING READ

I did an MA in creative writing in 2003-2004 and it felt like the only model offered for writing success was to get an agent and a publishing deal. Of course, things have changed since then, with the advent of e-books, self-publishing etc. But even then, with my own professional background in literature development (I had worked as a literature development officer in Leicester before leaving to do my MA) I had an inkling that there were other ways, not just of getting published, but of operating as a writer in the world.

This is another long story, but the bones of it are that I developed a writing practice that meant I was earning my living as a writer years before I got the publishing contract I had dreamed of for so long. And I was doing that, not through journalism or copy-writing, but through creative work which fed into, sustained, and indeed developed my novel writing.

How? Again it's complicated, but ultimately I make and take opportunities to do writing residencies and socially engaged arts projects which a) involve me working with diverse communities in diverse places and b) involve my own creative writing as well as facilitating and harnessing others' creativity and stories. You can have a look around my website – www.urbanwords.org.uk – to get a sense of the projects I have done over the last eight years or so. They have included writing children's books in collaboration with patients and carers at Great Ormond Street Hospital; creating co-authored work and my own new short stories with staff on the Central line, for Art on the Underground; writing poetry inspired by oral histories in east London – the poems were fabricated into poetic way-markers and installed along walking routes. I have spent many hours meeting new people, listening to their stories and finding new ways to tell them to a wider audience.

This kind of work isn't for everyone, but I love it. It keeps my eyes open to the world; it increases my understanding of people, place, politics, psychology; it allows me to share and work with my love for stories; it strengthens my novels. My last novel was told from the perspective of a seventeen-year-old boy. I don't think I could have written it – nor perhaps would I have come up with the idea for it – had I not spent years working with young people through my project work. My new novel is from the perspective of two octogenarians, inspired – I am sure – by a recent project working with older people in Preston.

Writing a novel is hard. It takes a long time. We do it because we love it, because we have to, because we have a story to tell. Getting a novel published is hard. I don't understand the market – I'm not sure anyone really does. Luck, craft, persistence, talent – they all play a role. All we can do is carry on, not give up, find ways to feed ourselves (literally and emotionally), and remember that we do not need anyone else's permission.

EXERCISE

Choose a character you are already working on and feel you know reasonably well. Now think about something they would never do. It can be big or small: they'd never travel alone; kill someone; stand up for themselves; do a bungee jump; quit their job; eat meat. Now write a scene where they do that thing and see what happens.

This was an exercise given to me by the aforementioned Emma Claire Sweeney. It gave me an image which I knew, as soon as I'd thought of it, was going to be the final scene of *Ten Things I've Learnt About Love*. I hope it's as productive for you.

TOP TIPS

- Write the best book you can. Keep that as your focus – above and beyond any ambition to get published, prove yourself, earn money. Make it about the story and the quality of the prose. Hold onto that.
- Don't give up (unless you want to, of course!). Find ways to keep yourself motivated and supported. The value lies in doing the writing – you're always learning and getting better. Hold onto that.

- Hemingway is often quoted as saying 'the first draft of anything is shit'. I concur. When you set out on a new project, don't worry about writing terrible sentences, flat characters, and improbable plot lines. Writing is a process. You have to sweat your way through the mire in order to get to the good stuff. Trust the process. Trust yourself. Hold onto that.

TEN BOOKS I LOVE

The White Family, Maggie Gee
When Rain Clouds Gather, Bessie Head
The Long Dry, Cynan Jones
English Passengers, Matthew Kneale
Unaccustomed Earth, Jhumpa Lahiri
Station Eleven, Emily St John Mandel
Jazz, Toni Morrison
Dept. of Speculation, Jenny Offill
Postcards, Annie Proulx
Honour, Elif Shafak

WILL WILES

PLOT TWISTS

I REMEMBER THE precise moment I realised that I wanted
to be a writer. I wish I could say that it came while reading
Nabokov or Ballard or DeLillo, but it did not. I was reading a novel by the late Michael Crichton, king of the tech-
no-thriller, in the heyday of his success, the early 1990s. It
wasn't even one of his best novels: not *Jurassic Park* (1990),
not *The Andromeda Strain* (1969), not *Sphere* (1987). I had
read all of those and was working my way through the 'By
the same author' page in that urgent, obsessive teenage way
that demands *ingestive* words: chewing, devouring, raven-
ing. This rampage through the Crichton back-catalogue had
reached *Congo* (1980), which concerns a disastrous expedition to find an diamond-infested El Dorado lost in the African
jungle.

This isn't very sophisticated or scientific, but let's divide
Crichton's oeuvre into three rough categories: good books
(chiefly those listed above); bad books (forgettable early pulp,
regrettable later crankiness); and books that can't be called
good but which I greatly enjoyed. *Congo* falls into that last
category and it's with surprise verging on astonishment that I

am obliged to admit – to myself as much as to you – that few other books have had such a profound influence on me.

My epiphany came towards the end of the book. The plot took a dramatic twist. I can't remember exactly what it was, either something to do with hot-air balloons or gorilla assassins. Whatever it was, it was exciting. Exciting is one of those formerly intense words that have been softened into a gentle, generic term of praise. But this was, for the teenage me, literally exciting in the purest sense: 'to cause to become active; to stir up; to rouse'. I was so excited I had to put the book down, rise from my chair, and walk around the room, propelled by a sudden surfeit of energy and joy. I was moved, actually physically moved.

I then stopped to think about what had just happened. I was an enthusiastic reader and this wasn't the first time a book had had a big effect on me – like I say, this wasn't even the best Crichton I had read. But the thought that a book, even a not-so-good book, could work my emotional state so effectively as to cause a physical outburst, that was interesting. I wanted to understand what Crichton had done, to figure out the trick. I knew that a literary mechanism had been used on me, and I wanted to dismantle that mechanism and examine its nuts and bolts. And I wanted to be able to make something like that myself, to create in readers some of the same emotion I had just experienced. I wanted to be a writer.

So how does the plot twist work? As well as being one of the most powerful literary mechanisms, it is also very possibly the oldest, older, in fact, than literature, and as old as story. Perhaps it is the basis of story itself – that we only devised plots in order to enjoy them being twisted. Certainly character and style only go so far in fiction, an observation as old as Aristotle. In *Poetics* (335 BCE), Aristotle wrote:

[I]f you string together a set of speeches expressive of character, and well finished in point of diction and thought, you will
not produce the essential tragic effect nearly so well as with a
play which, however deficient in these respects, yet has a plot
and artistically constructed incidents.

The most emotionally powerful of these incidents, Aristotle
continued, were *peripeteia* and *anagnorisis*. That's the only
Greek I'm going to bring into this, I promise. *Anagnorisis*
means 'recognition', or the moment when ignorance is replaced
by knowledge. Take one of the most brutal and original twists
in modern literary fiction, which comes at the climax of *The
Wasp Factory* (1984), Iain Banks's astonishing and transgres-
sive first novel. Is it necessary to warn you of spoilers? They
are, I'm afraid, unavoidable in this discussion – and perhaps
the most well-known feature of the plot twist is that it is unsat-
isfying to have the twist revealed in advance, or to be able to
guess it. Anyway, *The Wasp Factory*. Francis, the protagonist
(maybe that promise about Greek earlier was a mistake), is
an adolescent boy growing up on an isolated Scottish island.
Possessed by a murderous rage that he cannot sate and cannot
trace to its origin, he whiles away the days with inventive acts
of violence and cruelty. At the end of the novel he discovers the
truth: he is not Francis but Frances, born a girl, and still a girl,
albeit one mauled in a childhood accident and heavily dosed
with male hormones. Her circumstances have not changed,
but this revelation transforms her – and our – understanding
of everything that has gone before. And *The Wasp Factory*'s
revelation fits well into the classical tradition of *anagnorisis*,
in which the tragic hero discovers something about their true
nature: Oedipus discovers that Polybus and Merope are not
his parents and he has in fact murdered his father and married
his mother; Luke Skywalker learns that it's not Darth, it's Dad.

It doesn't have to be rooted in character; it can be almost any kind of revelation. It it doesn't even have to be a discovery by the protagonist, or any character in the story – the important person making the discovery is the reader, which is why spoilers and too-obvious twists are a bore.

Peripeteia means 'reversal of fortune', in particular *sudden* reversal of fortune. *A Song of Ice and Fire*, the fantasy series by George RR Martin, which has become the popular TV series *Game of Thrones*, is a particularly well known for its continual twists, and most of these twists take the form of *peripeteia*. Eddard Stark, the hero of the first of the series, suffers double *peripeteia*, first being cast into prison at precisely the moment he thinks he is bringing justice to the court, and then being executed when he thinks he is going to be pardoned in exchange for a false confession. Pretty much every single character suffers a major reversal of fortune at some point, particularly the few competent or honourable ones, often at the moment their competence or honour looks like it might actually achieve something positive in Martin's horrible world. But it happens to the evil characters too.

The classic(al) example of *peripeteia* – the example Aristotle cites – is, again, Oedipus. Upon learning that he has killed his father and bedded his mother, he is destroyed, becoming a maimed, pitiable creature. In the tale of Oedipus, *anagnorisis* and *peripeteia* occur pretty much simultaneously – one causes the other. And that, for Aristotle, was the key to the effective twist: revelation of truth and reversal of fortune working together. Modestly, I can illustrate this with an example from my own first novel, *Care of Wooden Floors* (2012), cleverly undermining any self-promotion advantage by ruining the plot. The protagonist is looking after a fastidious friend's much-prized apartment. He slightly damages the expensive, beautiful wooden floor and, fearing his friend's reaction, tries to put things right, only to unleash greater and greater disaster. In the end he is reduced to flipping the floorboards to conceal the damage – only to discover that the other side has already been damaged by his not-so-perfect friend. The floors are far too delicate and susceptible to staining to be practical; the friend has come to realise that the high standards he applies to the world are unrealistic; far from being angry, the friend is positively pleased that his little experiment has played out the way he expected. The protagonist is off the hook – but furious that he has been put through hell, and done terrible things, on the basis of little more than an intellectual prank.

Crucially, the reversal of fortune doesn't have to be negative, a fall: it can be an escape from apparently certain doom, or the snatching of victory from the jaws of defeat. Many of the most satisfying twists are positive. *Congo* ends on a double reversal. First, a volcano erupts, dooming everyone; then, the surviving characters realise that they have a hot-air balloon in their possession, and can escape.

That's not all there is to twists, of course. If you don't fancy tackling the cliff-face of two thousand years of global literary theory but still have several lifetimes to squander, take a look at the fractal, Borgesian library that is the TV Tropes database (tvtropes.org), where a tireless army of anonymous, dedicated popular-culture Linneans have assembled a seemingly endless and permanently proliferating catalogue of different kinds of twist. Some varieties of twist have only the faintest relationship to *anagnorisis* and *peripeteia*: the 'false protagonist' for instance, a kind of *peripeteia* practised on the reader. A good example of this is Toby Litt's fourth novel *DeadKidSongs* (2001), in which one of the reader's fundamental expectations is subverted by having a narrator die mid-story.

But the purpose here isn't to describe all twists but to explore what makes a good twist. And that means introducing one last concept: Chekhov's gun. This is named in honour of the Russian author and playwright Anton Chekhov, who observed that if you show a gun in the first act of a play, it must go off in the third. He was making a point about literary economy, stating that everything included in a story should be significant, even if that significance is only made clear much later, and that the insignificant should be excluded. This, like all literary rules, is debatable and open to exception. Consider, for instance, the red herring, which is like an inversion of Chekhov's gun: a plot object that appears to be significant, but is in fact insignificant, and serves only to draw the reader's attention away from what is truly significant.

It's this question of 'later significance' that makes Chekhov's gun an important feature of a good twist. We see the gun, register the presence of the gun, and when the gun later goes off are reminded of its first introduction. There's the real secret. A truly satisfying twist is one that brings new understanding while introducing a minimum of new information. In *The Wasp Factory*, 'Francis' is well aware of all the strange incidents and features of 'his' life and dwells on them constantly. It takes one crucial piece of missing information – that he is a she – to bring it all together into meaning. In Crichton's *Congo*, the characters had all the bits and pieces of the hot-air balloon with them all the time, found among the left-behind equipment of a previous expedition early in the story. They just didn't know what they were looking at. A good twist is like that hot-air balloon: all the components are right there in plain sight, but the reader doesn't know what they are looking at until the crucial moment.

Congo was the first time I looked at a twist for what it was, so it has personal significance, but I make no apology for resting so much of this essay on a blockbusting novel that doesn't have all that much 'literary' merit. Whatever Crichton's other qualities as a writer, he was a master of the twist – he built them with the precision of an aerospace engineer. The twist is one area where the 'popular', 'mainstream', 'commercial' novel has a vast quantity it can teach literary fiction. Iain Banks's own expertise at the twist was one of the factors that made him a bestseller as well as one of Granta's young darlings. It's possible to write a novel without twists. But why would you want to?

EXERCISE

Journalists at newspapers and magazines are taught to arrange news stories according to the so-called 'pyramid structure'. The first line of the story should contain the best possible summary of the story as a whole. Then, each subsequent line – each layer of the pyramid – adds a little more information, in order of the importance of that information. This means that the story is rigidly hierarchical, and if the newspaper sub-editors have to cut it to fit, their work is made easy: they can just cut from the bottom. It can be helpful to think of the outline for your story or novel this way, starting with a brief one-line summary, adding more, and then thinking about how your view of the story would change if a sub-editor was steadily cutting from the bottom. Which facts are important? Which are not?

TOP TIPS

- If you feel blocked, it's unlikely that the sentence or paragraph you're stuck on is the real cause of the trouble. It might be wrong, but it's not where you went wrong – that will almost certainly be earlier.
- Read non-fiction. Novels are great and all, but I find it's non-fiction that leads to ideas.

- Cook. Cooking is the mirror image of writing, its opposite and perfect companion. Cooking is haptic and sensual, writing is not. Cooking is begun and ended in an evening, writing is not. Cooking has very quick results compared to writing. Writing does not tend to directly benefit one's partner. You stand to cook and most of us do not stand while we are writing. And so on. There's no better way to end a day of writing than by cooking a meal. It rests the mind and fills the stomach. You'll write better.

TEN NOVELS WITH GREAT TWISTS

Fight Club, by Chuck Palahniuk (1996). Who is Tyler Durden? David Fincher's 1999 film of Palahniuk's first published novel has made the answer to that question common knowledge, but the original is still well worth your time for its structural inventiveness.

Use of Weapons, by Iain M Banks (1990). Many of Banks's novels have excellent twists. This science-fiction outing stands out among the field, not only for the horrifying surprise at the end, but also the expert way Banks weaves together galaxy-scale drama and intimate family secrets.

The Affirmation, by Christopher Priest (1986). Priest is another sure hand with the literary twist, and a number of his novels could be included in this list – *The Prestige*, for instance, which appropriately enough concerns the workings of a magic trick. But *The Affirmation*'s abrupt change of setting sticks in the memory.

The Machine, by James Smythe (2014). Any book dealing with the fallibility of memory is prime twist territory, especially so if those memories can be rewritten at will by a sinister black home appliance. And so it proves in this chilling vortex of a novel.

Money, by Martin Amis (1984). Perhaps Amis's best novel, and certainly his best-built twist. Exactly who is bankrolling the movie production that has propelled the loathsome John Self's sudden good fortune?

Eon, by Greg Bear (1985). More science fiction, but it is a genre that revels in revelations. A giant space habitat, apparently built by our descendants in the distant future, arrives in orbit around Earth. Mysterious enough – and then the reader discovers what's in its seventh chamber.

Meatspace, by Nikesh Shukla (2014). A witty and at times agonising novel about social media and assumed identity. Kitab Balasubramanyam, a young writer, is surprised when the only person on the internet who shares his name arrives on his doorstep. But it's the unexpected turn the novel takes near the end that gives the story genuine emotional ballast.

Notes on a Scandal, by Zoe Heller (2006). An account of an unwise love affair between a young teacher and one of her pupils, told from the point of view of the teacher's sympathetic older colleague . . . who, it transpires, is a textbook unreliable narrator.

The Lighthouse, by Alison Moore (2012). A man named Futh goes on a walking holiday to escape his imploding marriage, and reminisces about his past. It sounds so slight, but the conclusion of this haunting debut novel is shattering.

We Have Always Lived in the Castle, by Shirley Jackson (1962). Another exercise in unreliable narration, and an indisputable modern classic. The reclusive – indeed, pariah-like – Blackwood family have a great deal of secrets, some of which are pieced together amid Uncle Julian's confused autobiographical ramblings. But the biggest of them concerns the crime that has led to their present isolation.

GRAEME SHIMMIN

ON BEING BORING

'An author is a fool who, not content with boring those he lives with, insists on boring future generations.'
CHARLES DE MONTESQUIEU, Philosopher, 1689-1755

WELL DONE ON getting this far.
You've read this book, and applied its lessons. Your novel features realistic characters, and oozes profound wisdom from every paragraph. You've found your voice, and your prose is polished to gleaming perfection. So, you send it out to literary agencies, full of hope.

You get nothing but rejections.

What has gone wrong?

Well there's several possibilities. Publishers are notoriously drunk before breakfast for one thing. Literary agencies are staffed entirely by blonde women called Cressida who live in Chelsea for another. Maybe the world just isn't ready for your genius. But there's another possibility. Once we face up to it, we will get published and win the fame, riches and hot sex we deserve.

And I'm not exaggerating one little bit.

Because, we are going to examine the main problem with your novel: NOTHING FUCKING HAPPENS.

LEARN FROM THE GREATS

Lee Child. JK Rowling. Dan Brown. What do they have in common?

Yes, yes, I know, I hate them too. Lucky bastards, lying by the pool in Los Angeles writing their multimillion-selling . . . Oh, no, hang on, I'm just jealous. But why do people read their books? It's not the splendour of the language. It's not because they are masters of metaphor, punctuation or realistic characterisation. It's not because of their profound insight into the nature of society. Instead they have a special secret trick: STUFF HAPPENS.

Stories are about stuff happening. Without that, you have at best a vignette.

Okay, I know *something* happened in your novel. There was loads of stuff . . . There was that bit where . . . er . . . you know where that character, what's his name . . .

D'oh.

THIS NOVEL OPENS MORE SLOWLY THAN A BANK MANAGER'S WALLET

If only Cressida hadn't given up on your book after the first chapter and she'd read the whole thing! If she'd done that she'd have realised that it got going towards the end, but she never got there.

Why not? The thing was, she had a hundred manuscripts to read that day and your opening chapter wasn't grabbing her. You guessed it – because nothing happened.

She sees opening chapters all the time that do nothing

except introduce the characters and describe the setting. They have slow openings. They are boring.

Yes, I know many classics have glacial openings. *Anna Karenina*, take a bow. But here's the thing: you aren't Tolstoy, and it isn't 1878 any more.

To make sure the opening isn't boring, open with the inciting incident, the event that kicks the plot off. You can feed those background details you were opening with in later.

MORE PADDING THAN A SUMO WRESTLER

So let's say Cressida has got past the first chapter. What stops her next?

Waffle. Aimlessness.

The length of a commercial novel is generally eighty to a hundred thousand words. That's a lot of words. And we didn't have enough plot to fill half that much novel.

So what did we do? We padded the story out with some random stuff that didn't have anything much to do with the story. We told ourselves we were exploring our protagonist's world. We wrote a sub-plot concerning her brother's unfortunate choice of marriage partner. The protagonist spent two pages travelling to meet the antagonist and feeling a tad nervous. We claim to be revealing her personality. We slipped in that chance meeting with an oddball traffic warden.

This is what we call a digression. Digression is boring. Because although something is happening, it's not relevant and so it just feels like . . . padding. You can trust your readers to fill in the gaps more than that. Because of television, they are very used to arriving late into a scene and swiftly orientating themselves.

To avoid digression and padding, we ask ourselves, 'What's the point of this scene and what is it adding?' We need to do this *for every single scene.* If any scenes add nothing then we need to think of relevant stuff to happen instead. Then each scene will add to the novel. And if the result of each scene is to set up a later one then the momentum will build and build.

IF I WANTED TO LISTEN TO A
SERMON I'D GO TO CHURCH

So, you want your book to make a point. That's great. In fact it's vital. As *Lajos Egri said in The Art of Dramatic Writing:* 'No idea and no situation was ever strong enough to carry you through to its logical conclusion without a clear-cut premise.' But storytelling is the *demonstration* of truth, not its explanation.

'A story's event structure is the means by which you first express, then prove your idea . . . without explanation.'
Robert McKee, Story

Sometimes, instead of *demonstrating* the premise, the narrator or one of the characters *explains* it. The story becomes heavy handed and preachy. Preachy is not fun because it abandons the core of storytelling – stuff happening.

TAKING A DUMP

In many novels there are what I call table-polishing scenes.

In a table-polishing scene, two characters tell each other stuff they already know to help the reader understand too. Sometimes they also polish the table.

If you have any of your characters saying to each other, 'As you know, Bob . . .', 'Remember, chaps . . .', or, 'Tell me, professor . . .', then you have a table-polishing scene.

Don't do this – Cressida thinks it's boring.

The other boring way of doing exposition is the info-dump. Cressida sees this one all the time, even from published writers who really ought to know better. The story stops. The author coughs politely. They step forward and deliver a two-page monologue on police procedures, the ecology of the alien homeworld and how to cook squid.

Then the novel resumes, probably without Cressida, who has put the manuscript on her desk and gone to make a cup of tea.

The way to avoid this problem is to set up characters with reasons to discuss the plot. With different views on what to do. They confront each other about the best way forward.

Then the reader picks up the information without even realising it.

THE TWELVE-YEAR-OLD TEST

There's nothing more boring than being confused about what is happening. Nothing, that is, except not even being able to understand what the author is trying to say.

The average reading age of the British population is nine, that is they've achieved the reading ability that wildly optimistic educationalists expect from a nine-year-old. This, I'm afraid, is what society has come to. And attention span? The average attention span is . . . oh look at that shiny thing . . . uh, sorry, what was I saying? Yeah, about that long.

I blame television.

There's a scientific measure of how readable your work is. It's called the Flesch-Kincaid test. In the seventies, the United States Navy asked scientists to discover why no one could understand their technical manuals. The scientists discovered that multisyllabic words were demanding to peruse. After

years of effort, they chanced upon another stunning revelation, discovering that interminable, byzantine sentences, which
like this sentence are often full of sub-clauses, though perhaps
demonstrating something about the mindset of the author, and
being redolent of their intellectual prowess, and despite being
favoured by classical authors such as Herman Melville, who
famously wrote many sentences over a hundred words long,
are hard to follow too.

That doesn't mean you can't write attractive sentences.
You know what? Focussing them might even improve them.
Shorter sentences are clearer sentences. They have subordinate
clauses, adverbs and adjectives trimmed out. They are punchy.
Remember, Hemingway won the Nobel Prize for Literature
writing punchy prose.

So, remember, scientific research has conclusively proven
that people don't think you're clever just because you use big
words. So edit for clarity as well as style. This is what I call the
twelve-year-old test.

And I'm not talking about whiskey.

BUT . . . BUT . . .

Okay, okay, I can sense the angry reader fuming. Because being boring, like being posh, is something no one will admit
to. Here's a couple of things I sometimes hear: 'If those bozos
can't follow my book that's their problem. They must be stupid.' And, My book is not *boring*, it is *serious*.'

Well, that's fine, and there's some truth in those arguments.
Whether your novel bores your readers depends on whether
it meets the reader's expectations. And no one expects a high-
level, literary novel to have the same level of narrative drive as
a spy thriller.

It's also true that what engages one reader doesn't engage

another. Some people want 'to see what happens'. Others find themselves more engrossed by the characters. Non-stop action can become nearly as boring as non-stop talking.

But the only thing Cressida cares about is whether she can sell your book to a publisher for enough money to pay the mortgage on her compact and bijou flat in Chelsea. And the main thing the publisher is concerned with, apart from where his wife hid the gin, is how many copies your novel will sell. So, considering that the vast majority of readers can't and won't read something boring, my question is, do you want to get your book published?

EVERYTHING IS COMING UP ROSES

So there's Cressida at the end of a long day. She has summarily rejected ninety-eight boring novels already. And the next one on her pile is yours. She sighs and picks it up.

Something interesting happens on the first page. So she reads the first chapter. The writing is crisp and clear. Each scene is interesting. She's engrossed. She knows she probably ought to go home, but she thinks she'll just read one more chapter . . .

EXERCISE

Write down:
   Where your story takes place (SETTING).
   Who your main character is (PROTAGONIST).
   What they're trying to do (PROBLEM).
   Who's or what is stopping them (ANTAGONIST).
   What major obstacle the protagonist faces (CONFLICT).
   What they hope to achieve (GOAL).

Use that information and the Killogator™ logline generation formula below to write a one- or two-sentence logline for your story:

In a (SETTING) a (PROTAGONIST) has a (PROBLEM) (caused by an ANTAGONIST) and (faces CONFLICT) as they try to (achieve a GOAL).

(For tips on using the formula, google 'Killogator'.)

TOP TIPS

- You have to realise the first draft isn't the end. You need to write at least three drafts before you even attempt to find an agent or publisher. There will be at least three more drafts if they buy your book.
- Keep learning and improving. Read all the classic examples of the kind of novel you want to write, buy books about writing techniques, do creative writing courses, join critique groups, online and in real life, and really listen to your feedback. Learning is the key difference between eventual success and ongoing failure in my opinion. Everyone always says not to give up, and it's true that you shouldn't, but you have to get better too.
- Network. Commercial publishing is a relationship business. You either have to know people or be extremely lucky if you want to get commercially published. How do you network though? Start with other authors. Support each other. Help each other. They move in the circles you need to get into.

TEN NOVELS THAT ARE NOT BORING

The Riddle of the Sands, Erskine Childers
Greenmantle, John Buchan
The Mask of Dimitrios, Eric Ambler

Rogue Male, Geoffrey Household
From Russia With Love, Ian Fleming
The Day of the Jackal, Fredrick Forsyth
The Spy Who Came in From the Cold, John le Carré
The Hunt For Red October, Tom Clancy
Fatherland, Robert Harris
Pattern Recognition, William Gibson

You can read in-depth reviews of all those novels on my website, graemeshimmin.com.

CONTRIBUTOR
BIOGRAPHIES

JENN ASHWORTH's first novel, *A Kind of Intimacy*, won a
Betty Trask Award in 2010. On the publication of her second,
Cold Light, she was listed by the BBC's *The Culture Show*
as one of the UK's twelve best new writers. Her third novel,
The Friday Gospels, is currently being adapted for television.
She teaches creative writing at Lancaster University and is one
of the co-founders of Curious Tales, a writer-led performance
and publishing collective.

TOM BROMLEY is the author of twenty books: two novels,
two novellas (under the pseudonym Thomas Black), six works
of non-fiction and ten ghostwritten titles, ranging from bestselling autobiographies to books on everything from econom-
ics to JRR Tolkien. A former commissioning editor, editorial
director and publisher, he teaches novel and genre writing for
the Faber Academy.

SARAH BUTLER explores the relationship between writing
and place through prose, poetry and participatory projects.
Recent writing residencies include writer-in-residence on the
Central line; at Great Ormond Street Hospital; and *Tideline*
– a public art project linked to a major regeneration project
in Belvedere, East London. She has two novels published by

Picador: *Ten Things I've Learnt About Love* and *Before The Fire* www.sarahbutler.org.uk www.urbanwords.org.uk

AJ DALTON is an international author with Gollancz Orion. His novels include *The Book of Orm*, *Empire of the Saviours*, *Gateway of the Saviours*, and *Tithe of the Saviours*. He currently teaches Creative Writing at Manchester Metropolitan University, and lives with his cat Cleopatra. He was born in Croydon. He maintains the website www.ajdalton.eu.

STELLA DUFFY has written thirteen novels, over fifty short stories, and ten plays. She has twice won Stonewall Writer of the Year and twice won the CWA Short Story Dagger. She adapted her novel *State of Happiness* for film with Zentropa/Fiesta; HBO have optioned her Theodora novels for a TV mini-series. Also a theatre-maker, she is Associate Artist with Improbable and Artistic Director of Shaky Isles Theatre. She is the Co-Director of Fun Palaces, the campaign for greater engagement for all – in all culture. www.funpalaces.co.uk

KERRY HUDSON was born in Aberdeen. Her first novel, *Tony Hogan Bought Me an Ice-Cream Float Before He Stole My Ma*, was published in 2012 by Chatto & Windus and was the winner of the Scottish First Book Award while also being shortlisted for the South Bank Sky Arts Literature Award, Guardian First Book Award, Green Carnation Prize, Authors' Club First Novel Prize and the Polari First Book Prize. Her second novel, *Thirst*, was published in 2014.

TOBY LITT grew up in Ampthill, Bedfordshire. He is the author of four collections of stories and eight novels. His latest book of stories is *Life-Like*, published by Seagull Press. Toby's completion of Neil Gaiman's graphic novel, *Free Country: A*

Tale of the Children's Crusade, is due from Vertigo in September 2015. He teaches creative writing at Birkbeck College. His website is at www.tobylitt.com.

LIVI MICHAEL is the author of six novels for adults and twelve for children. *Succession*, (Penguin Random House, 2014) is the first part of a trilogy about the Wars of the Roses and *Rebellion* (Penguin Random House 2015) is its sequel. She teaches Creative Writing at Manchester Metropolitan University.

JAMES MILLER was born in London in 1976. He is the author of two novels – *Lost Boys* and *Sunshine State* – and numerous short stories. With a PhD in African-American Literature and Civil Rights, he teaches creative writing at Kingston University.

ALISON MOORE was born in Manchester in 1971. She is the author of two novels – *The Lighthouse* (2012), shortlisted for the Man Booker Prize and the National Book Awards and winner of the McKitterick Prize, and *He Wants* (2014) – and a short story collection, *The Pre-War House & Other Stories* (2013). She lives near Nottingham with her husband Dan and son Arthur.

MARK MORRIS has written over twenty-five novels, including *Toady*, *Stitch*, *The Immaculate*, *The Secret of Anatomy*, *Fiddleback*, *The Deluge* and four books in the popular Doctor Who range. He is also the author of two short story collections, *Close to the Bone* and *Long Shadows, Nightmare Light*, and several novellas. His short fiction, articles and reviews have appeared in a wide variety of anthologies and magazines, and he is editor of *Cinema Macabre*, a book of horror movie essays by genre luminaries for which he won the 2007 British Fantasy Award, its follow-up *Cinema Futura*, and *The Spectral Book of Horror Stories*.

LEONE ROSS is a Jamaican/British award-winning writer, editor and lecturer. She is the author of two novels, *All the Blood is Red* (Angela Royal Publishing) and *Orange Laughter* (Anchor), and numerous magic realist, horror and erotic short stories. She won an Arts Council award in 2001, and, in 2013, her short story collection, now entitled *Come Let Us Sing Anyway*, was shortlisted for Salt's Scott Prize. She works as a senior lecturer at the University of Roehampton in London and her third novel, *This One Sky Day*, is forthcoming.

NICHOLAS ROYLE teaches English at the University of Sussex, where he is director of the Centre for Creative and Critical Thought and convenor of the MA in Creative and Critical Writing. He has published numerous books, including *Telepathy and Literature: Essays on the Reading Mind* (1991), *EM Forster* (1999), *The Uncanny* (2003), *How to Read Shakespeare* (2005) and *Veering: A Theory of Literature* (2011). In collaboration with Andrew Bennett, he is also author of *Elizabeth Bowen and the Dissolution of the Novel* (1995), *This Thing Called Literature* (2015) and *An Introduction to Literature, Criticism and Theory* (5th edition, 2016). His novel, *Quilt*, appeared in 2010.

GRAEME SHIMMIN was born in Manchester, and studied Physics at Durham University. His successful consultancy career enabled him to retire at 35 to an island off Donegal and start writing. He has since returned to Manchester and completed an MA in Creative Writing. His first novel, *A Kill in the*

Morning, won the YouWriteOn book of the year award, was shortlisted for the Terry Pratchett Prize and subsequently was published by Transworld.

NIKESH SHUKLA is the author of *Meatspace*, the Costa First Novel Award-shortlisted *Coconut Unlimited* and the Sabotage Reviews Best Novella winner *The Time Machine*. He is the host of The Subaltern Podcast and Dumsnet. He wrote *Kabadasses*, a comedy lab pilot for Channel 4 in 2011 and the award-winning short film, *Two Dosas*, based on his short story of the same name. His short stories have appeared in the *Sunday Times*, *Best British Short Stories 2013*, *Too Much Too Young*, *Teller Magazine*, *Litro* and *Five Dials*, and been broadcast on BBC Radio 4. He lives in Bristol.

JOE STRETCH is the author of three novels – *Friction* (2008), *Wildlife* (2009) and *The Adult* (2012), for which he won the Somerset Maugham Award. His 'Choose Your Own Adventure' audiobook, *Don't Let Go*, was read by Anna Friel, published by Spotify and received a Cannes Lion Award in 2011. His debut film, *Wizard's Way*, received several awards and was optioned for remake by Jack Black. His band, Performance, released two albums. Their songs have appeared in film and television around the world. He lectures at Manchester Metropolitan University.

ALICE THOMPSON was born and brought up in Edinburgh. She was the keyboard player with post-punk eighties band The Woodentops and joint winner, with Graham Swift, of the James Tait Black Memorial Prize for Fiction for her first novel, *Justine*. Her second novel, *Pandora's Box*, was shortlisted for the Stakis Prize for Scottish Writer of the Year. Her other novels are *Pharos*, *The Falconer*, *The Existential Detective* and, most recently, *Burnt Island*. Alice Thompson is Lecturer in Creative Writing at Edinburgh University.

WILL WILES is the author of *Care of Wooden Floors* (2012), which won a Betty Trask Award, and *The Way Inn* (2014), which was shortlisted for the Encore Award. His next book is called *Plume*. When not writing novels he works as an architecture and design journalist. He lives in London.